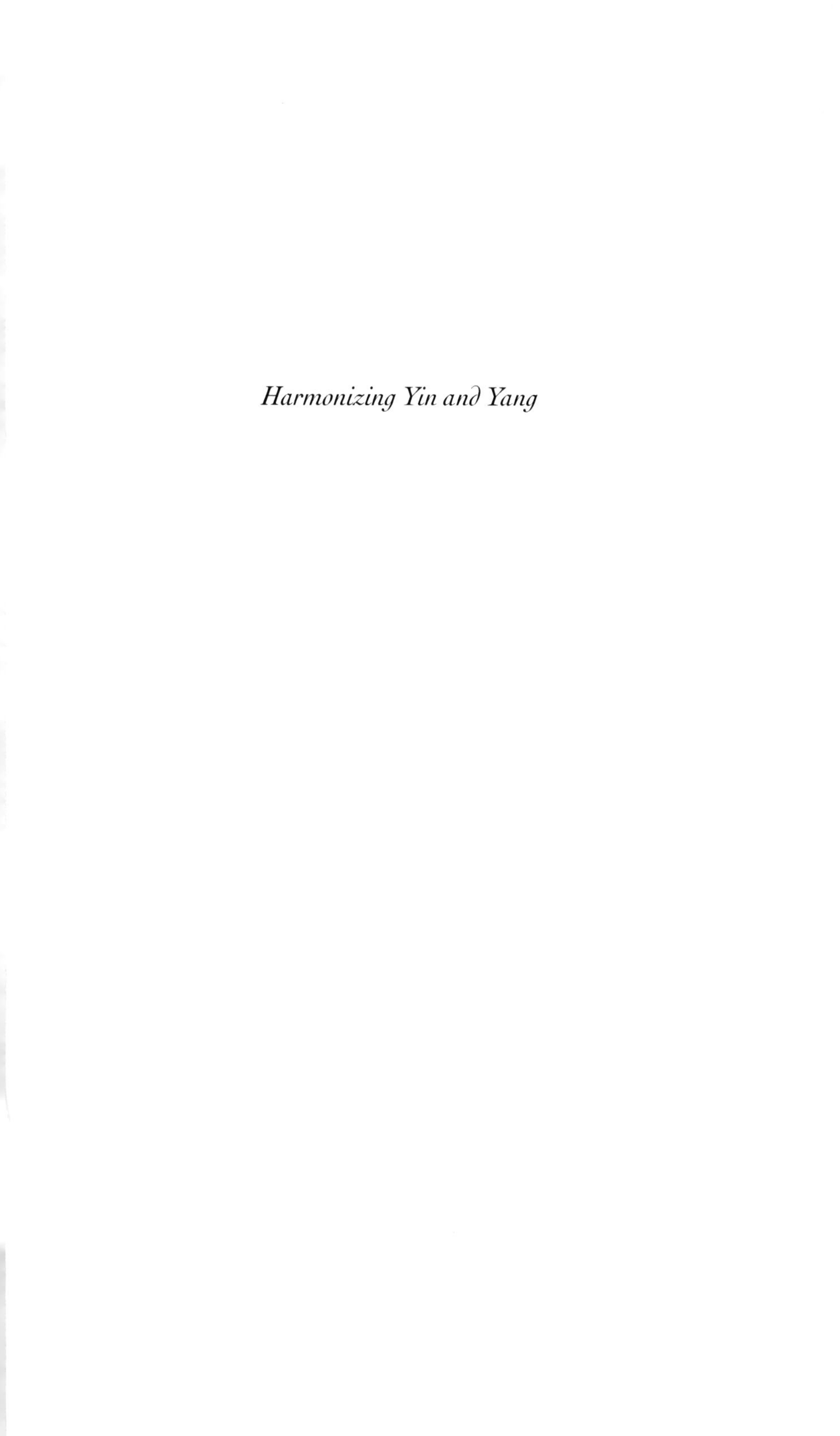

Harmonizing Yin and Yang

Harmonizing Yin and Yang

The Dragon-Tiger Classic

Translated and with an introduction by Eva Wong

SHAMBHALA
Boston & London
1997

Shambhala Publications, Inc.
Horticultural Hall
300 Massachusetts Avenue
Boston, Massachusetts 02115
www.shambhala.com

Printed in the United States of America

∞ This edition is printed on acid-free paper that meets the American National Standards Institute Z39.48 Standard.

♻ Shambhala Publications makes every effort to print on recycled paper. For more information please visit us at www.shambhala.com.

Distributed in the United States by Random House, Inc., and in Canada by Random House of Canada Ltd

Library of Congress Cataloging-in-Publication Data

Lung hu ching. English.
Harmonizing yin and yang: the Dragon-tiger classic / translated and with an introduction by Eva Wong.—1st ed.
p. cm.
ISBN 978-1-57062-306-6 (pbk.: alk. paper)
1. Taoism—Sacred books. 2. Alchemy—Religious aspects—Taoism. 3. Yin-yang. I. Wong, Eva, 1951– . II. Title.
BL1900.L88E52 1997 97-2435
299'.51482—dc21 CIP

Contents

Part Three

Harmonizing Yin and Yang

Introduction

A Guide to Reading the Dragon-Tiger Classic

To age with the sun and moon and be renewed by spring and summer, to conserve the seeds of growth in autumn and winter and to be nourished by the eternal breath of the Tao—these are the goals of the Taoist alchemists, the masters of the arts of health, longevity, and immortality.

Taoist alchemy is also concerned with spiritual transformation. This transformation involves changing the body and mind from a mundane state to one that mirrors the timeless and permanent reality of the Tao. Alchemy is said to be the most challenging and dangerous path of Taoist spiritual practices. If the endeavor is successful, the alchemist can attain longevity and immortality in his or her own lifetime. If it fails, illness, mental derangement, and even death can result.

The Chinese arts of health and longevity are the products of centuries of experimentation, research, and development. Those of us who practice the techniques of internal transformation today are grateful to the Taoist alchemists for their efforts in searching for the elixir of immortality. True, the idea of immortality has changed, and now immortality no longer means eternal life on earth. But without the efforts of the early alchemists, herbal and traditional Chinese medicine, ch'i-kung, Taoist calisthenics, the internal martial arts, and Taoist meditation would not have achieved the kind of sophistication they exhibit today.

This book is a translation of the *Dragon-Tiger Classic* and its two most important commentaries. The texts are collected in the T'ai-hsüan ("Great Mystery") section of the Taoist canon published during the reign of the emperor Cheng T'ung (1436–1449 CE) of the Ming dynasty (1368–1644 CE).

About the Dragon-Tiger Classic

The *Dragon-Tiger Classic* is regarded by contemporary practitioners of Taoist alchemy to be the most complete guide to spiritual transformation. It describes the ingredients, the catalysts, the equipment, the nature of the physiological transformations, and, most important, the schedule of the firing process needed to initiate the alchemical interactions. All this information is encoded in a set of mnemonics of 1,293 words, making the *Dragon-Tiger Classic* one of the most challenging alchemical treatises to understand. That so much information is packed into so few words does not mean that there is little to say about the transformations. Rather, it is characteristic of Taoist alchemical treatises to reveal only partial information, and even then, in symbolic language. Since the basic information was general knowledge among the community of practitioners and instructions for advanced adepts were transmitted orally, Taoist alchemical treatises often leave out the most basic and the most advanced information. This arrangement worked well as long as there was an active community of practitioners. However, as practitioners dwindled, knowledge not written down was lost.

Given the complexity of the alchemical processes described in the *Dragon-Tiger Classic* and the amount of background information needed to understand the text, I have written a "reader's guide" for it. Unless you are extremely familiar with the theory and practice of Taoist alchemy, I would urge you to read this introduction before you tackle the text and the commentaries.

My own understanding of the *Dragon-Tiger Classic* was helped tremendously by my practice of the Taoist alchemical arts. It has allowed me to reconstruct missing information and unravel the multiple layers of meanings encoded in the text.

The authorship of the *Dragon-Tiger Classic* is unknown. The version in the Cheng-t'ung Taoist canon was edited by two Sung dynasty (960–1279 CE) Taoists, Wang Tao and Chou Chen-i, who also added comments in parts of the Secondary Commentary. Wang Tao considered the *Dragon-Tiger Classic* one of the oldest known texts of Taoist alchemy, possibly written before the Eastern Han dynasty (25–220 CE). However, Chu Hsi, the Sung dynasty neo-Confucianist philosopher, argued that the text was written much later, probably during the T'ang dynasty (618–906 CE). At present, there is no agreement about when the *Dragon-Tiger Classic* was written. The authorship of the Primary Commentary is also unknown, and there is no information about when it was written. All we can say is that it could not have been written earlier than the second century CE because it contains extensive references to the *Tsan-tung-chi* (Triplex Unity), the alchemical classic of the Eastern Han. The Secondary Commentary was most likely a work of the Sung dynasty because it contains ideas that were characteristic of the internal-alchemical treatises of that period.

Three levels of meaning are encoded in the *Dragon-Tiger Classic*. The original text can be read simultaneously as a manual of external, sexual, and internal alchemy. The Primary Commentary can be read as a manual of both sexual and internal alchemy, and the Secondary Commentary is best read as a manual of purely internal alchemy. To understand these three levels of meaning, we need to first familiarize ourselves with the three forms of Taoist alchemy—external, sexual, and internal.

The Three Forms of Taoist Alchemy

External Alchemy

In external alchemy, practitioners ingest substances to attain health, longevity, and immortality. The idea that plants, metals, and minerals could enhance health and help mortals attain immortality dates back to China in the fourth century BCE. However, the belief that certain minerals and metals have life-giving and transforming properties goes back as far as the eighth or ninth century BCE. The Chinese have always admired the beauty and indestructibility of metals such as gold and silver. Thus it was not surprising that these metals became the symbols of an indestructible and immortal corporeal body. Red ochre and red cinnabar were also valuable substances in ancient China. They were used to make the red pigment that adorned oracle bones and sacred ceremonial objects. The ancient Chinese believed that the color red was associated with blood and life, and that substances with that natural color embodied the essence of life. That cinnabar can be transformed into quicksilver, or mercury, made it even more magical and mysterious.

By the second century BCE, when the belief in immortals became the center of social and intellectual life among the court and the nobility, the search for methods of attaining immortality began. The emperors of both the Ch'in (221–207 BCE) and the Han (206 BCE–219 CE) dynasties employed researchers, called the fang-shih, to find or make a substance that, if ingested, could make them immortal. Some fang-shih experimented with plants and herbs and became the precursors of Chinese herbal medicine. Others entertained the idea that if substances like cinnabar, gold, and mercury were made "potable" and ingested, they could make the human body indestructible and immortal. The fang-shih reasoned that if the right metals and minerals were compounded in the correct way, a pill or an elixir of immortality would materialize. Thus external alchemy was born. The principal alchemical ingredients were mercury, lead, cinnabar, and silver; the equipment needed for refining the substances were a furnace, a cauldron, and bellows; and the procedures for heating and compounding the substances were patterned after the movement of the sun, moon, and stars, and the cycle of the seasons. The elixir of immortality was called the lung-hu ta-t'an, or the Great Dragon-Tiger Elixir.

The attempts at making elixirs and pills of immortality by

compounding metals and minerals flourished in China from the third century BCE to the tenth century CE. By the eleventh century CE, external alchemy lost its momentum. Twelve hundred years of research and experimentation had failed to produce an elixir of immortality. Moreover, people became skeptical of external alchemy when they saw many patrons and proponents die of lead and mercuric poisoning. Today we would not consider eating substances like mercuric sulphide, lead, quicksilver, or cinnabar, but the belief in ingesting minerals to attain health and longevity is still around—one need only look at the list of minerals on the bottles of vitamin and diet-supplement pills.

Read as a text of external alchemy, the *Dragon-Tiger Classic* is a manual for compounding metals and minerals to produce the Great Dragon-Tiger Elixir, which, when ingested, can make an individual immortal. In the text, the dragon is cinnabar and mercury, and the tiger is lead. The chamber of the spirit is the cauldron where mercury is extracted from cinnabar and then compounded with lead to produce the elixir of immortality. The alchemical ingredients are sealed in the cauldron and are subjected to heating and cooling. The trigram k'an (☵) is water and the trigram li (☲) is fire, and applying k'an and li refers to regulating water and fire in the refining and compounding of the minerals and metals. The schedule of applying fire and water is called the firing process, and it is patterned after the cycles of the waxing and waning of yin and yang energies in nature. When the period of tempering is complete, a liquid (the elixir) or a powder (the pill), called the Great Dragon-Tiger Elixir, will materialize in the cauldron.

For more information on external alchemy, see Joseph Needham's *Science and Civilization in China*, vol. 5:2 (New York: Cambridge University Press, 1974).

Sexual Alchemy

In sexual alchemy, also known as "paired practice," the practitioner uses the energy of the sexual partner to cultivate his or her own. Sexual alchemy was practiced by Taoist alchemists as early as the first and second centuries CE. Just as the copulation of the sky (yang) and earth (yin) energies gave birth to humanity and the myriad things of the world, the union of the yin and yang, female and male, is the basis of creating and renewing the energy of life in the body.

Generative or procreative energy was recognized as life energy as early as the seventh century BCE. The early medical texts, including the *Huang-ti nei-ching su-wen* (Yellow Emperor's Classic of Internal Medicine) and the *Ling-shu* (The Spiritual Pivot), had counseled people to conserve ching, or procreative energy, for health. However, it was the Taoist alchemists who turned "the conservation of energy" into the "cultivation and gathering of energy." In sexual alchemy, the practitioner uses the generative energy from a sexual partner to stimulate and replenish his or her own. Pragmatics, not pleasure or romantic love, govern the practice of sexual alchemy. The classics of Taoist sexual alchemy repeatedly tell practitioners to treat their partners only as a source of energy and not to have feelings of pleasure or love while energy is being gathered. Otherwise, energy will be lost rather than cultivated.

In Taoist sexual alchemy, the union of male and female energies is crucial in producing the elixir of immortality in the body. The ingredients of the alchemical interactions are the procreative energies of the sexual partners; the equipment consists of the bodies of the partners; and the firing schedule refers to the phases of the waxing and waning of the female and male procreative energies in the body.

Read as a text of sexual alchemy, the *Dragon-Tiger Classic* and the Primary Commentary are manuals on how to gather and use sexual energy from a partner to cultivate one's own regenerative energy. The tiger is lead, and lead is the essence of male generative energy hidden in the female. This energetic structure is represented by the trigram k'an (☵), which consists of a yang component (the solid line) surrounded by two yin components (the broken lines). The dragon represents mercury and cinnabar. Mercury is the liquid generative energy hidden in the male. This energetic structure is represented by the trigram li

(☵), which consists of a yin component surrounded by two yang components. Mercury, a liquid, symbolizes the volatile sexual energy that can escape and flow out of the body if not contained. On the other hand, cinnabar, a solid, is sexual energy in its stabilized form that stays inside the body to become the seed of immortality. In the *Dragon-Tiger Classic,* the union of the tiger and the dragon refers to the union of the male in the female (the tiger or lead) and the female in the male (the dragon or mercury/cinnabar). It is not simply the union of male and female. Otherwise, the trigrams ch'ien (sky ☰) and k'un (earth ☷) would have been used instead of k'an and li.

According to the *Dragon-Tiger Classic,* the tiger and dragon are drawn out of k'an and li and united when fire and water are applied. Applying external fire means using the sexual partner to stimulate the production of generative energy within the recipient. Regulating the water refers to the production of generative energy within the recipient when the sexual organ is aroused. In the text and the Primary Commentary, the procreative energy is manifested as drops of "liquid pearl," the clear fluid that is secreted when sexual arousal is first experienced. If this liquid is contained and absorbed into the body along with the generative energy of the partner, it will be transformed into the elixir of immortality. The container where the energies are held and transformed is the chamber of the spirit inside the cauldron. The cauldron consists of an upper and a lower crucible, which are the bodies of the sexual partners, and the chamber of the spirit is the place where the male and female sexual organs are joined.

In sexual alchemy, it is crucial that the gathering and cultivating of generative energy occur when the generative energies are at their height. Thus the schedule of the firing process is based on the cycles of the waxing and waning of yang and yin generative energies in both the female and the male. The effects of sexual alchemy are optimal when both the female and the male procreative energies are at their height. Therefore the texts of sexual alchemy advise practitioners to gather energy only at certain times of the day, month, and year. Otherwise, not only will the quality of the energy gathered be low, but the recipient will not be able to utilize the energy optimally.

Although the manuals of sexual alchemy were written primarily from the perspective of male adepts, the practice of sexual alchemy is not restricted to men. Female practitioners can gather energy from a sexual partner by withdrawing the energy into the body just before an orgasm. The female intentionally directs the energy back into her body when she feels that an orgasm is about to occur. Thus the energy is not released in her orgasm but is absorbed back into her body along with the "pearls" of the male to form the elixir of immortality.

For more information on Taoist sexual alchemy, see Douglas Wile's *The Art of the Bedchamber* (Albany: State University of New York Press, 1992).

Internal Alchemy

In internal alchemy, the ingredients and equipment of the alchemical process are entirely contained in the practitioner's own body. The physiology is changed from within, without the aid of herbs, minerals, or energy from a sexual partner.

Internal alchemy rose from the death throes of external alchemy. During the late T'ang and the early Sung dynasties, the Taoists realized that it was futile to make a pill or an elixir of immortality from minerals and metals. Gradually they turned to techniques that transformed the body from within. Absorbing the influences of Zen and T'ien-tai Buddhism and neo-Confucianism, Taoists such as Lü Tung-pin, Wang Ch'ung-yang, and Chen Hsi-yi advocated the simultaneous cultivation of mind and body. They developed techniques of meditation, calisthenics, and yogic postures to transform the body and the mind and to circulate internal energy. Some internal alchemists, like Chang Po-tuan (the author of the *Wu-chen p'ien* [Understanding Reality] and patriarch of the Southern School of Complete Reality Taoism), also practiced sexual alchemy. Others, like Ch'iu Ch'ang-ch'un (a student of Wang Ch'ung-yang and one of the Seven Taoist Masters), were against the use of sexual techniques in gathering energy. Ch'iu Ch'ang-ch'un's form of internal alchemy dominated the Taoist arts of longevity from the late Sung onward; and during the Ming (1368–1644) and Ch'ing (1644–1911) dynasties, internal alchemy became synonymous with techniques of spiritual transformation that do not make use of "external" substances, be they herbs, minerals, or energy from a sexual partner.

Read as a text of internal alchemy, the *Dragon-Tiger Classic* and its two commentaries contain instructions for transforming and harmonizing the yin and yang energies in the body. The dragon and mercury refer to vital energy in the middle t'an-tien, a field of energy located around the solar plexus. It is the yin energy hidden in the fires of the heart (li). The tiger and lead refer to generative energy in the lower t'an-tien, a field of energy centered around the navel. It is the yang energy hidden in the waters of the kidneys (k'an). The copulation of the dragon and the tiger, mercury and lead, water and fire, refer to the different dimensions of the union of yin and yang energies in the body.

In internal alchemy, applying fire means using the breath to fan the fires of the lower t'an-tien and circulate the internal energy (or ch'i). The firing process therefore refers to the applications of warm slow fire (yin fire) and fast hot fire (yang fire). The warm slow fire is used to gather the yin and yang energies and the fast hot fire is used to refine and transform them. The schedule of the firing process describes the optimal time for applying the yin and yang fires, and this schedule is based on the rise and fall of yin and yang energies in the body's biological cycles. The equipment of internal alchemy—furnace, cauldron, and crucibles—is the t'an-tien in the body. The furnace is the lower t'an-tien, where the internal fires are generated. The cauldron is the container where internal energy is gathered, refined, and transformed. Internal alchemists recognize three cauldrons—upper, middle, and lower, which are associated with the refinement and transformation of the spiritual, vital, and generative energies respectively. Finally, the pill or elixir of immortality is the primordial energy of the Tao that emerges in the body of the internal alchemist when the refined yin and yang energies are united.

For more information on internal alchemy, see my book *The Shambhala Guide to Taoism* (Boston & London: Shambhala Publications, 1997).

The Alchemical Interactions of Yin and Yang in the Dragon-Tiger Classic

The alchemical transformations described in the *Dragon-Tiger Classic* are concerned with the union of yin and yang. Regardless of whether the text is read as a manual of external, sexual, or internal alchemy, understanding the nature of the ingredients, the alchemical equipment, the alchemical interactions, and the schedule of the firing process is crucial to deciphering the text and the commentaries.

The Ingredients

The key ingredients of alchemy are symbolized by the trigrams k'an (☵) and li (☲). When these two interact, the yin and yang energies are united. As mentioned earlier, the interaction is between the yang in the yin and the yin in the yang, not simply yin and yang. The yang hidden in the yin (symbolized by the solid middle line in the trigram k'an) copulates with the yin hidden in the yang (symbolized by the broken line in the middle of the trigram li) to activate the alchemical processes that will produce the Golden Elixir or Pill of Immortality.

K'an (☵)

In the *Dragon-Tiger Classic,* k'an is described as water, moon, the Great Yin, yin, north, the Black Tortoise, the numeric six of the celestial stem wu of earth, and the Celestial Stems jen and kuei of the north (see figure 1 for a list of the Celestial Stems, their yin and yang affiliations, and their associated elements and directions). K'an embodies yang, which is hidden in the center of the trigram. Therefore water has in it the energy of fire. The yang in the yin is described as the White Tiger, the

Celestial Stem	*Direction*	*Yin/Yang*	*Element*
chia	east	yang	wood
i	east	yin	wood
ping	south	yang	fire
ting	south	yin	fire
wu	center	yang	earth
chi	center	yin	earth
keng	west	yang	metal
hsin	west	yin	metal
jen	north	yang	water
kuei	north	yin	water

Terrestrial Branch	*Direction*	*Yin/Yang*	*Element*
tzu	north	yin	water
ch'ou	northeast	yin	water
yin	northeast	yang	water
mao	east	yin	wood
ch'en	southeast	yin	wood
ssu	southeast	yang	wood
wu	south	yin	fire
wei	southwest	yin	fire
shen	southwest	yang	fire
yu	west	yin	metal
hsü	northwest	yin	metal
hai	northwest	yang	metal

Figure 1. The ten celestial stems and twelve terrestrial branches with their associated direction, yin/yang affiliation, and element. The twelve months of the year and the twelve two-hour segments of each day are named after the terrestrial branches. Note that the celestial stem wu is different from the wu of the terrestrial branch. When wu and chi are mentioned together, the wu refers to the celestial stem. When wu is mentioned with tzu, the wu refers to the terrestrial branch. Also note that the terrestrial branch yin is different from the yin of yin and yang.

metal of the west (black lead, silver, white gold, yellow gold), the essence (or spirit) of the sun, and the middle son of the trigram ch'ien (☰). Thus *the essence of a substance is found in its complementary opposite.*

Throughout the text, the following expressions are used to describe the yang in the yin:

The essence of yin is yang.
The essence of water is fire.
The energy of water is fueled by fire.
The essence of the female is male.
The essence of the moon is the sun.
The moon gets its light from the sun.
The spirit of the sun is in the moon.
The light of the moon comes from the Celestial Stem wu of earth.
The White Tiger is born in the water of k'an.
The White Tiger is the essence of the moon.

Li (☲)
In the *Dragon-Tiger Classic,* li is described as fire, sun, the Great Yang, yang, south, the Red Raven, and the numeric six of the Celestial Stem chi of earth. Li embodies yin, which is hidden in the center of the trigram. Therefore fire has in it the energy of water. The yin in the yang is described as the Green Dragon, cinnabar and mercury, the wood of the east, the mysterious water, the essence (or soul) of the moon, and the middle daughter of the trigram k'un (☷). Again we find the essence of the alchemical ingredient in its complementary opposite.

Throughout the text, the following expressions are used to describe the yin in the yang:

The essence of yang is yin.
The essence of fire is water.
The energy of fire is fueled by water.
The essence of the male is female.
The essence of the sun is the moon.

The sun gets its light from the moon.
The soul of the moon is in the sun.
The light of the sun is from the Celestial Stem chi of earth.
The Green Dragon is born in the fire of li.
The Green Dragon is the essence of the sun.

It is the natural attraction between the opposites that allows the Green Dragon in li and the White Tiger in k'an to be united. When the yang in the yin is united with the yin in the yang, the Golden Elixir of Immortality is produced. However, although the ingredients are inherently compatible, they need to be drawn out of hiding and gathered in a place where they can copulate and be harmonized. This is where the alchemical equipment comes into play.

The Alchemical Equipment

The principal piece of alchemical equipment described in the *Dragon-Tiger Classic* is the cauldron. The cauldron consists of an upper and a lower crucible. In the text, the upper crucible is called the dome or the lid and the lower crucible is the bowl where the ingredients are collected. The upper crucible is patterned after ch'ien, the sky, and the lower crucible is patterned after k'un, the earth. The cauldron itself is made of white metal (white gold), which is transformed from black lead. Enclosed in the cauldron is the chamber of the spirit. This is where the vapor of earth will harmonize and unite the yin and yang energies. It is the one cubic inch of emptiness where the elixir of immortality is created. These three components of the cauldron—upper crucible, lower crucible, and chamber—are symbolized by the general structure of the three lines that make up a trigram. In the trigram, the top line represents the upper crucible and the bottom line represents the lower crucible. The middle line is called the harmonious middle because the chamber is where the vapor of harmony gathers the yin and yang energies. (The structure of the alchemical equipment as described in the *Dragon-Tiger Classic* is illustrated in figure 2.)

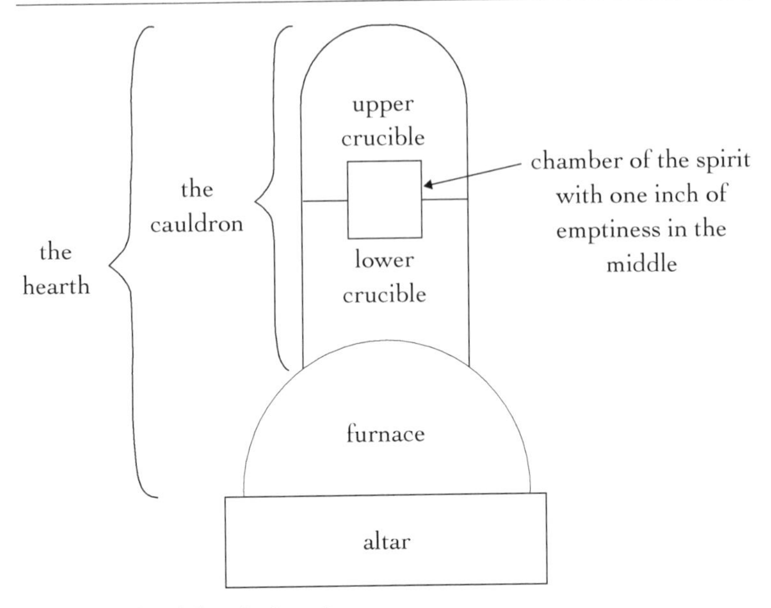

Figure 2. The alchemical equipment.

The Alchemical Interactions and Transformations

The Nature of the Alchemical Interactions

As mentioned earlier, the alchemical interaction is between the yang in the yin (the White Tiger) and the yin in the yang (the Green Dragon). In this interaction, the White Tiger and the Green Dragon are transformed into numinous energy and united to form the Golden Elixir. The yang component in k'an moves into li to occupy the middle position, and the yin component in li is drawn into the center of k'an. The first process is described as using k'an to fill li, refining the silver in the lead, extracting the white metal from the water of the north, and returning the essence of the sun to the empty hollow of the moon. The second process is described as playing with the Red Raven, extracting the mercury from the fire, and refining mercury from cinnabar. The interaction itself is referred to as the Green Dragon copulating with the White Tiger, or the soul of the moon embracing the spirit of the sun.

The key to the interaction between the Green Dragon and White Tiger is in getting the hidden yin and the hidden yang to come out and embrace each other. There is a natural attraction between the two, but catalysts are needed to draw them out of hiding and refine them. The catalysts are water and fire, and herein lies the complexity of the meanings of k'an and li. K'an and li are used to describe both pre-creation (or Earlier Heaven) and post-creation (or Later Heaven) water and fire. In the realm of pre-creation, delineated by the pre-creation pa-k'ua (see figure 3), k'an is in the west and li is in the east. East is associated with the element wood and west is associated with the element metal. Thus the Green Dragon is referred to as the wood of the east and the White Tiger is referred to as the metal of the west. This is why it is said that water in the west gives birth to the metallic White Tiger and fire in the east gives birth to the mercuric Green Dragon. In the realm of post-creation, delineated by the post-creation pa-k'ua (again, see figure 3), k'an is in the north and li is in the south. North is associated with water and south is associated with fire. Therefore the Black Tortoise is referred to as the water of the north and the Red Raven is referred to as the fire of the south.

When you read the *Dragon-Tiger Classic*, it is important not to confuse the pre-creation and post-creation dimensions of k'an and li. The k'an and li of pre-creation are associated with the White Tiger and the Green Dragon, which are the alchemical ingredients. The k'an and li of post-creation are associated with the Black Tortoise and the Red Raven, which are catalysts. In the alchemical interaction, post-creation water (k'an) and fire (li) are applied to pre-creation metal (which is in k'an) and wood (which is in li) to extract the hidden elements. This is what the *Dragon-Tiger Classic* means when it says, "Externally, fire and water interact; internally, wood and metal subdue each other."

Effects of the Alchemical Interactions

When the yang in the yin interacts with the yin in the yang, several transformations occur. Hidden substances (like the

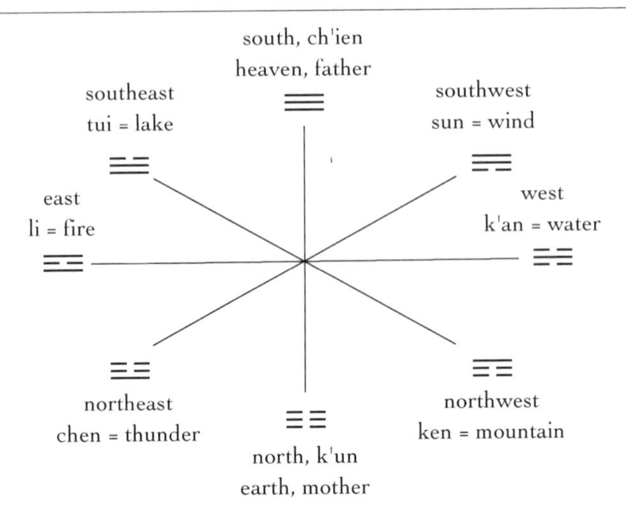

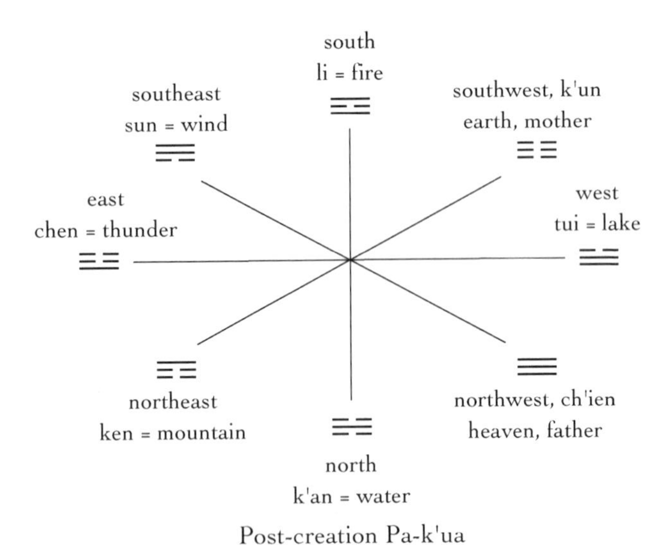

Figure 3. The pre-creation (or Earlier Heaven) and post-creation (or Later Heaven) pa-k'uas. Notice that in the pre-creation pa-k'ua, li and k'an occupy the east-west axis, and in the post-creation pa-k'ua, they occupy the south-north axis. Also note that in the Chinese compass, south is positioned on top and north at the bottom.

White Tiger and the Green Dragon) are extracted, emerging substances (lead and mercury) are refined, and new substances (golden nectar and Golden Elixir) are created.

The following is a list of alchemical interactions described in the *Dragon-Tiger Classic*. Note that the interactions and transformations occur simultaneously, although each is discussed separately below.

1. *When the yang in k'an moves to the middle position of li, lead emerges and crude cinnabar is extracted from the lead. When the yin in li moves to the middle position of k'an, mercury is extracted from crude cinnabar.* In the first process, water is used to draw the yang out of k'an. In the second process, fire is used to draw the yin out of li. (Recall from an earlier discussion that in ancient metallurgy, mercury is a product of cinnabar, and cinnabar is mined along with metals such as lead.) Thus, in this alchemical transformation, three substances—lead, cinnabar, and mercury—are extracted. This alchemical process is also described as the sun and moon copulating. When li (sun) and k'an (moon) embrace, the sun (the Great Yang) produces mercury or the mysterious water, which is the yin energy embodied in the yang; and the moon (the Great Yin) produces yellow gold or the true lead, which is the yang energy embodied in the yin.

2. *The wood of mercury creates the Green Dragon and the essence of metal nourishes the White Tiger.* When the fire of li (the Red Raven) is circulated, the mercuric dragon will be drawn out of li to copulate with the "mother of metal," the White Tiger. When the water of k'an (the Black Tortoise) is circulated, the metallic tiger will be drawn out of k'an to copulate with the "father of mercury," the Green Dragon, which is cinnabar. Note that yang fire (Red Raven) is used to extract the yin (Green Dragon) from the yang (li), and that the Green Dragon is the "father," *not* the mother, of mercury. Likewise, water, which is yin fire, is used to extract the yang (White Tiger) from the yin (k'an), and that the White Tiger is the "mother," *not* the father, of metals. This alchemical interaction reminds us that there is yin in yang and yang in yin, and the interactions involve

unraveling the tangle of mundane yin and yang energies and reuniting them in their primordial pattern.

3. *When water is applied to metal, sacred water, or numinous mercury, emerges to create the golden nectar. When fire is applied to metal, the celestial stems wu and chi emerge to create the powder of cinnabar. When wood encounters metal, the spirit emerges.* Golden nectar, powder of cinnabar, and spirit are different manifestations of the elixir of immortality. The golden nectar is the elixir in liquid form; the powder of cinnabar is the elixir in the form of a pill or crystal; and the spirit is the primordial breath of the Tao. These interactions all describe the action of water and fire (two catalysts) and wood (a substantive ingredient) on metal, which is the White Tiger.

4. *When li and k'an copulate, cinnabar and mercury are transformed.* First, when the middle yang component is drawn out of k'an, raw cinnabar, a solid, or yang, substance is transformed into quicksilver (or mercury), a yin, or liquid, substance. This refers to mercury being extracted from its root substance, the crude cinnabar. The inert and solid yang within the yin now becomes a volatile liquid. This liquid is the essence of yang energy and will dissipate quickly if left in this form. Thus, in the second transformation, when the middle yin component is drawn out of li, quicksilver, the liquid yin substance, is transformed into powdered cinnabar, a solid yang substance. This transformation stabilizes the volatile mercury so that it can be contained and made into cinnabar powder or the immortal pill.

5. *The arousal of ch'ien (pure yang energy) produces li, and the arousal of k'un (pure yin energy) produces k'an.* In the emergence of li, the Green Dragon (mercury) is created. In the emergence of k'an, the White Tiger (lead) is created. Pure energy is dormant. Here ch'ien and k'un refer to the yang and yin energies in us when we were in our mother's womb. Before contact with the world, these energies are not attracted to each other. However, after birth, contact with the world arouses the ch'ien and k'un energies and transforms them respectively into their hybrid forms, li and k'an. Li and k'an are attracted to each other because the yin in the yang and the yang in the yin "long" to

return to their original state. This natural attraction between li and k'an forms the basis of the alchemical reunion of the yin and yang energies and their return to their original prenatal or primordial state.

Taoist alchemy is fundamentally involved with bringing together opposites and compounding them to form the elixir or pill of immortality. The opposites are brought together by the element earth, the "agent of harmony" that resides at the center of the macrocosmic and microcosmic universe. Figure 4 summarizes the alchemical interactions and transformations described above.

The Sequence of Transformations in the Chamber of the Spirit
According to the *Dragon-Tiger Classic,* the principal alchemical transformations occur in the chamber of the spirit in the caul-

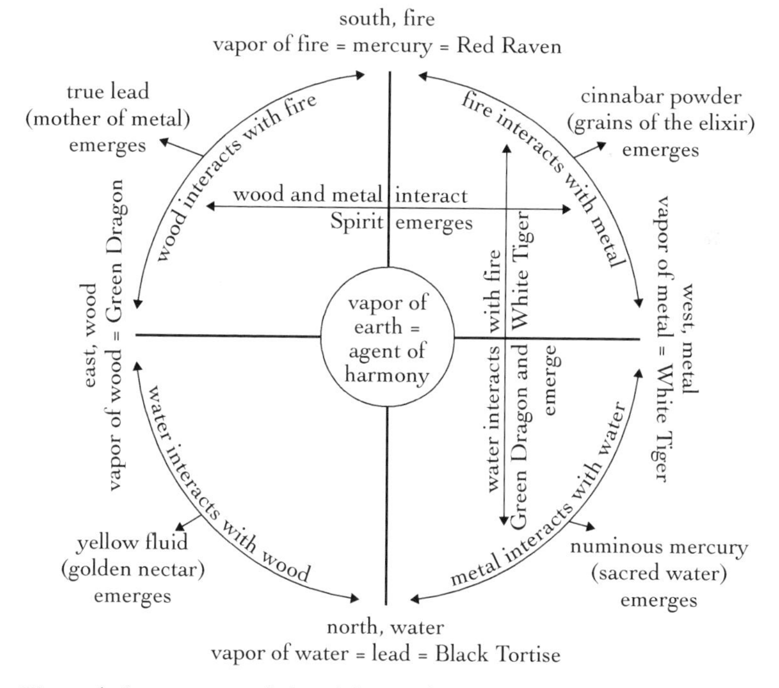

Figure 4. A summary of the alchemical interactions described in the *Dragon-Tiger Classic.*

dron. (Refer to the section "The Alchemical Equipment" for a review of the structure of the cauldron.) Once the upper and lower crucibles are in place and the elements are gathered inside, water (warm, or yin, fire) is applied to extract the metal (the yang in the yin) from k'an (hybrid yin energy). Black lead, which is hidden inside k'an, emerges. Fire (hot, or yang, fire) is then applied to the black lead to transform it into white metal. The white metal is used to build the chamber of the spirit within the cauldron. When yang fire is applied again, white metal is transformed into a liquid silver, which rises to become the golden nectar. The lead sinks and becomes the powder of cinnabar. The Golden Elixir of Immortality, in both its liquid (nectar) and solid (powder) form, is now complete.

The Firing Process

According to the *Dragon-Tiger Classic,* the firing process is the key to making the elixir of immortality. The schedule of applying the yin and yang fires is patterned after the trigrams and hexagrams of the *I Ching*. Yin fire is the warm slow fire that circulates downward in a counterclockwise manner. It is used to gather the ingredients and harmonize the opposites. Yang fire is the hot fast fire that circulates upward in a clockwise manner. It is used to transform the collected ingredients into new substances.

The yin and yang components of the trigrams and hexagrams describe the nature of the fire applied. The composition of the trigrams and hexagrams therefore tells us the type of fire used. For example, the trigram ch'ien (☰) indicates that the fire should be three parts yang, and the trigram k'un (☷) indicates that the fire should be three parts yin.

There are at least two schedules of firing, and they occur simultaneously as parallel processes. The first one is patterned after the trigrams, and the second one is patterned after the hexagrams. In addition, there are several unique events in the firing process that are described by special hexagrams.

The Trigram Level of the Firing Process

To understand the schedule of the firing process at the level of the trigrams, look at figure 5. First you will notice that six of the eight trigrams in the pa-k'ua are used to describe the schedule of firing. These trigrams are chen (☳), tui (☱), ch'ien (☰), sun (☴), ken (☶), and k'un (☷). The remaining two, k'an and li, are not used to describe the schedule of firing

	Days	Trigram	Hours	Anchor Day
first half of the month: yang fire waxes, yin fire wanes	new moon first 5 days	☳ chen	tzu 11 PM–1 AM ch'ou 1–3 AM	3rd day moon rises in keng, west
	second 5 days	☱ tui	yin 3–5 AM mao 5–7 AM	8th day moon rises in ting, south
	third 5 days full moon	☰ ch'ien	ch'en 7–9 AM ssu 9–11 AM	15th day moon rises in chia, east
second half of the month: yin fire waxes, yang fire wanes	fourth 5 days	☴ sun	wu 11 AM–1 PM wei 1–3 PM	16th day moon rises in hsin, west
	fifth 5 days	☶ ken	shen 3–5 PM yu 5–7 PM	23rd day moon rises in ping, south
	sixth 5 days	☷ k'un	hsü 7–9 PM hai 9–11 PM	30th day moon rises in i, east

Figure 5. The trigram level of the firing process. The anchor day is when the fire reaches its target temperature. You will notice that the anchor day falls in the middle of a phase, except on the fifteenth and sixteenth days (around the full moon). In these two phases, the fires build up, reach their target temperature, and diminish within one day.

because they represent the two types of fire (yin and yang) used. Chen, tui, and ch'ien describe the ascending movement of the hot and fast yang fire; and sun, ken, and k'un describe the descending movement of the warm and slow yin fire. The cycle of yang fire begins with chen, the trigram that has one yang component at the bottom. This is the "first fire of yang" or the "birth of yang." In the scheme of the *I Ching,* yin and yang are said to "grow" from the bottom up. A trigram with a yang line at the bottom is said to be one in which yang is waxing, and a trigram with a yin line at the bottom is said to be one in which yin is waxing. Thus the trigram chen is often described as the first emergence of yang. When yang fire first starts to circulate, it is weak. However, with time, it gradually increases its strength. The next phase in the ascent of yang fire is described by the trigram tui, which is two parts yang and one part yin. Here the yang fire is stronger, but it is in ch'ien that the yang fire is at its height. The full amount of yang fire is represented by the three yang components of that trigram. After yang fire has reached its height, yin fire arrives. Its first appearance is described by the trigram sun, which has a yin component at the bottom. This indicates that yin is beginning to wax. It is delineated by the yin spreading from the bottom to push out the yang. (This condition is different from the trigram tui, which is also two parts yang and one part yin. There the two yang lines are at the bottom, indicating that yang is waxing and about to push out the yin line on the top.) Yin continues to wax in the trigram ken until it reaches its height in k'un. At k'un, the yin fire is pure because the trigram is three parts yin. After k'un, chen arrives, and the cycle begins again.

The second thing you will notice in figure 5 is the timing of the firing process. Yin and yang fires are applied on a daily as well as a (lunar) monthly cycle. The daily cycle is divided into twelve segments of two hours each. The cycle of yang fire begins at the hour of tzu (11:00 P.M. to 1:00 A.M.) and ends at ssu (9:00 to 11:00 A.M.). The cycle of yin fire begins at wu (11:00 A.M. to 1:00 P.M.) and ends at hai (9:00 to 11:00 P.M.). The monthly cycle is divided into two halves. Each half of the lunar month is subdivided further into three periods of five days each. In the first half of the month, yang fire waxes and yin fire wanes. In the second half of the lunar month, yang fire wanes and yin fire waxes. At the end of the month, the yin fire is at its height. When the new moon arrives the next month, yang fire is about to begin again.

The Hexagram Level of the Firing Process

In the hexagram level of the firing process, twelve hexagrams are used to describe the schedule of applying the yang and yin fires. Figure 6 shows how the firing process is patterned after the hexagrams. The first thing you will notice in figure 6 is that, as in the trigram level, the hexagrams associated with the waxing of yang fire all have yang components at the bottom and the hexagrams associated with the waxing of yin fire all have yin components at the bottom. Thus the yin and yang components of the hexagrams fu, lin, t'ai, ta-ch'uang, kuai, and ch'ien describe the nature of yang fire and the components of k'ou, tun, pi, kuan, po, and k'un describe the nature of yin fire.

The hexagram level of the firing process is more complex than the trigram level, although the logic behind both levels is similar. There are two cycles in this firing schedule. First, the yang and yin fires are applied sequentially in a daily, monthly, bimonthly, and yearly cycle. Second, the yang and yin fires are applied simultaneously in different schedules in a monthly cycle.

Figure 7 summarizes the sequential application of the yang and yin fires at the hexagram level. For completeness, the trigram level is also included in the figure so that you can get a full picture of the different levels of the firing process.

To appreciate the simultaneous application of the yang and yin fires, look at figure 8. You will notice that the two schedules are "staggered," that is, the periods of the yin and yang fires do not coincide. My belief is that the sequential schedule describes the application of the yang and yin fires at the global level, while the simultaneous schedule is concerned with the movement of the yang and yin fires at the local level. Based on personal experience in the practice of internal alchemy, I feel that the sequential schedule is involved with the waxing and waning of the yin and yang fires in the major pathways, and the simultaneous schedule is associated with the circulation of fire in the minor pathways in the body.

Hexagrams That Describe Special Events in the Firing Process

Several unique hexagrams are used to describe special conditions in the firing process. These hexagrams are tun (䷂), mong (䷃), wei-ch'i (䷿), and chi-ch'i (䷾). (Note that the "tun" here is different from the "tun" (䷠) in the group of hexagrams associated with the hexagram level of the firing process.)

The first pair, mong and tun, describes the application of fire to water. Here water is not yin fire but the fluid of generative energy in the body. According to the *Dragon-Tiger Classic,* tun governs the manner in which fire is applied to generative water in the first half of the day (between the hours of tzu and ssu). The hexagram tun consists of the trigrams k'an at the top and chen at the bottom. Recall from the discussion of the trigram level of the firing process that chen designates the first emergence of yang fire. Thus tun describes the application of weak or small amounts of yang fire to water or generative energy. The hexagram mong governs the manner in which fire is applied to generative water in the second half of the day (between the hours of wu and hai). It consists of k'an (water) at the bottom and ken at the top. Thus mong describes the condition where yin fire descends to interact with water or generative energy.

The second pair of hexagrams, wei-ch'i and chi-ch'i, describes a condition referred to in the *Dragon-Tiger Classic* as "the harmonious yang." This is delineated by the patterns of the two hexagrams. Wei-ch'i has li on top and k'an at the bottom, and chi-ch'i has k'an on top and li at the bottom. They both describe the condition in which the amounts of yin and yang energies are balanced. The *Dragon-Tiger Classic* identifies this condition

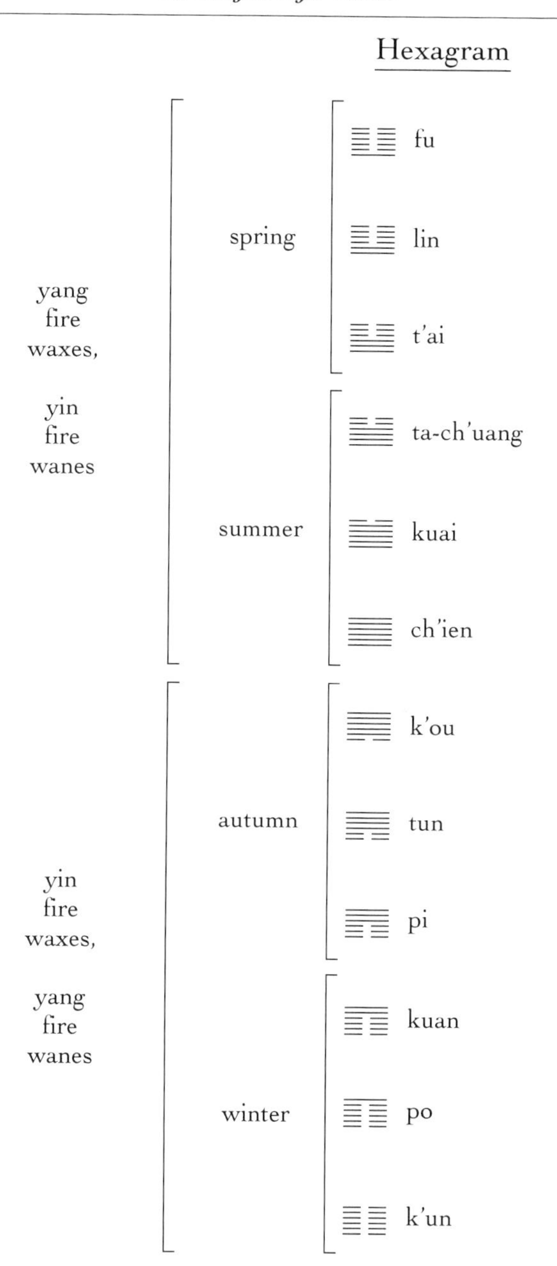

Figure 6. The hexagram level of the sequential firing process.

Levels of Cycles in the Firing Process

ascent of yang fire

Hexagram	Trigram	Hour	Direction	Day	Month	Days of the Month	Bi-month	Year
䷗ fu	☳ chen	tzu	N	first half of the day–morning	new moon 1st 5 days 1–5	1, 2, 3	1st 15 days of 1st month	winter solstice 1st quarter spring
䷒ lin		ch'ou	NE			4, 5		
䷊ t'ai	☱ tui	yin	NE		2nd 5 days 6–10	6, 7		
䷡ ta-ch'uang		mao	E			8, 9, 10	2nd 15 days of 1st month	2nd quarter summer
䷪ kuai	☰ ch'ien	ch'en	SE		3rd 5 days 11–15 full moon	11, 12, 13		
䷀ ch'ien		ssu	SE			14, 15		

descent of yin fire

<table>
<tr><td>䷫ k'ou</td><td rowspan="2">☴ sun</td><td>wu</td><td>S</td><td rowspan="6">second half of the day–evening</td><td rowspan="2">4th 5 days
16–20</td><td>16, 17, 18</td><td rowspan="3">1st 15 days of 2nd month</td><td rowspan="3">3rd quarter autumn</td></tr>
<tr><td>䷠ tun</td><td>wei</td><td>SW</td><td>19, 20</td></tr>
<tr><td>䷋ pi</td><td rowspan="2">☶ ken</td><td>shen</td><td>SW</td><td rowspan="2">5th 5 days
21–25</td><td>21, 22, 23</td></tr>
<tr><td>䷓ kuan</td><td>yu</td><td>W</td><td>24, 25</td><td rowspan="3">2nd 15 days of 2nd month</td><td rowspan="3">4th quarter winter</td></tr>
<tr><td>䷖ po</td><td rowspan="2">☷ k'un</td><td>hsü</td><td>NW</td><td rowspan="2">6th 5 days
26–30
no moon</td><td>26, 27</td></tr>
<tr><td>䷁ k'un</td><td>hai</td><td>NW</td><td>28, 29, 30</td></tr>
</table>

Figure 7. Levels of cycles in the sequential firing process.

Yang Fire Schedule

Hexagram	*Days of the lunar month*
fu	9–13
lin	14–18
t'ai	19–23
ta-ch'uang	24–28
kuai	29–3
ch'ien	4–8

Yin Fire Schedule

Hexagram	*Days of the lunar month*
k'ou	6–10
tun	11–15
pi	16–20
kuan	21–25
po	26–29 (or 30)
k'un	1–5

Figure 8. The hexagram level of the simultaneous firing process.

as occurring on the ninth day of the lunar month. Again, water here refers to generative energy. In the context of sexual alchemy, fire refers to male generative energy and water refers to female generative energy. In the context of internal alchemy, water is generative energy and fire is vital energy.

These, then, are the major ideas of Taoist alchemy described in the *Dragon-Tiger Classic* and its two commentaries. You will notice that the alchemical language and symbols can be interpreted differently depending on whether the text is read as a manual of external, sexual, or internal alchemy. As mentioned earlier, the original text is equally open to all three levels of interpretation. The Primary Commentary can be read as a manual of sexual and internal alchemy, and the Secondary Commentary is best understood from the perspective of internal alchemy.

The best way to read the *Dragon-Tiger Classic* is to allow the different levels of meaning to present themselves. Try to "listen" to the "voices" of the text and the two commentaries. Each has its own way of speaking and presenting itself. The original text is poetic, the Primary Commentary is didactic, and the Secondary Commentary is partisan. The introduction should only be used to familiarize yourself with the general ideas of Taoist alchemy. Once you are comfortable with the language of alchemy and have an understanding of its theory and practice, you should read the text again. This time, do not analyze it or refer to the introduction, or even look at the translator's notes. If you are receptive, the text will reveal its hidden meanings to you.

Although the *Dragon-Tiger Classic* was originally written as a manual for the three forms of Taoist alchemy—external, sexual, and internal, I would suggest that you do not use it as such. Unsupervised practice of the Taoist alchemical arts is dangerous. Physical and mental injuries can result if the techniques are practiced incorrectly. If you want to learn the Taoist alchemical arts, you should look for a teacher or a keeper of this traditional knowledge to instruct you. The goal of this book is to introduce an obscure area of Taoist knowledge to the noninitiated but interested reader. It is not meant to be an instruction manual. If this book gives you an appreciation of the Taoist techniques of spiritual transformation, or stimulates your interest in the Taoist arts of longevity, it will have more than accomplished its modest objective.

Part One

1

The Chamber of the Spirit Is the Pivot of the Elixir

The chamber of the spirit is the pivot of the elixir. It is the mother and father of all minerals. It is the secret residence of cinnabar and mercury.

Primary Commentary

The chamber of the spirit is the pivot of the elixir.

The chamber of the spirit is patterned after ch'ien (sky) and k'un (earth). It can gather the essence of the sun and moon to make the golden nectar of the sacred elixir. Therefore it is called the pivot of the elixir. The *Tsan-tung-chi* (Triplex Unity) says, "Ch'ien and k'un stand at the gateway of change."

It is the mother and father of all minerals.

The true lead was there before sky and earth were born. It is the father who created all things and the mother who nourished them. Therefore it is called the mother and father of all minerals. The *Tsan-tung-chi* says, "It is the mother and father of all the hexagrams."

It is the secret residence of cinnabar and mercury.

Cinnabar and mercury originally do not have form or substance. They are hidden within the true lead. They emerge in the chamber of the spirit only when they receive the pure essence of the sun. Therefore the chamber of the spirit is called the secret residence of cinnabar and mercury.

SECONDARY COMMENTARY

In the beginning, the Great Ultimate (t'ai-chi) transformed the primordial vapor into sky and earth, separated yin from yang, and created the sun and the moon. Humanity was placed in the middle, between sky and earth. Thus the Three Domains (celestial, terrestrial, and humanity) came into existence. It is said that of all creatures, humanity has the gift of intelligence. Therefore it can be the leader of the ten thousand things.

In the ancient times, people easily lived for a hundred or a thousand years. However, since the times of the Yellow Emperor, the human life span has shortened considerably. This is because people are no longer connected with the movement of the primordial vapor. As a result, they die or are injured. Sky and earth, however, can exist for millennia because they are continually nourished by the greatness of the pure and original vapor. Following the cycle of the four seasons, they create and dissolve the five elements and move naturally in their paths. The wise ones of old observed the pattern of the skies and understood the movement of the stars. They merged with the primordial vapor of nature and used it to nourish their bodies. Therefore their longevity was like that of the sky and the earth. Today people are different. The young ones crave sensual pleasure before the energy in their blood is fully developed. The old ones lose energy in their blood and are weakened by illnesses associated with aging. When they recognize their problems, it is too late. Only those who know how to preserve themselves will live a long life.

The enlightened ones were in harmony with changes in the

sky and the earth. They built the furnace and set up the cauldron to make the sacred medicine. When old people take this medicine, generative energy will be collected, the spirit will be gathered, and they will return to the vitality of youth. When young people take this medicine, they will attain immortality. The sage Chen-i likened the cultivation of the sacred elixir to the creation of sky and earth. The process can be described by the metaphors of change. The foundations of the Great Elixir are built on the roots of the earth. The method of making the Great Elixir is coded in the reverse movement of ch'ien and k'un. The application of fire and water is patterned after the trigrams li (fire) and k'an (water). Punishment and reward are given during the times of mao and yu.

Steal the numerics of movement from the four seasons and hold them in the palm of your hand. Use the workings of yin stillness and yang movement to create winter and summer. Yin gives birth to the fire star of the Red Raven constellation and yang creates the Mysterious Void. In movement, the lower component of the hexagram k'un is transformed on the ninth day of the lunar month. In stillness, ch'ien returns to the lower component of the hexagram on the sixth day. This is *the* key to cultivating the elixir.

Translator's Note

Mao and yu are times when water is accumulated and fire is stopped. During this time, the alchemical catalysts are not applied, so that the ingredients can be "bathed" or "soaked" in the standing vapor. The extent to which the ingredients can benefit from the "soaking" depends on the effects of yang and yin fires applied in the other periods of the firing process. This is why mao and yu are referred to as the times when punishment and rewards are given. If the yin and yang fires are regulated correctly, the practitioner will be rewarded with success. If the fires are applied incorrectly, the practitioner will meet with failure (or punishment). Figures 5 and 7 in the introduction show when mao and yu occur in the firing process.

2

Yang Exits and Yin Enters

Yang exits and yin enters. They flow and light up the two directions. Three is their number, and they are patterned after water and fire.

Primary Commentary

Yang exits and yin enters. They flow and light up the two directions.

Yang is born in the hour of tzu. Emerging from the earth, it waxes through the hours of ch'ou, yin, mao, ch'en, and reaches its zenith at ssu. Therefore the essence of the sun in the Green Dragon is brightest in the east. Yin comes in the hour of wu and enters the earth. It waxes through the hours of wei, shen, yu, hsü, and reaches its zenith at hai. Therefore the essence of the moon in the White Tiger is brightest in the west.

Three is their number, and they are patterned after water and fire.

The Green Dragon and the White Tiger are formed from the hot vapor of the Red Raven. Therefore it is said that there are three entities. In the process of making the Great Elixir, no substances other than the true lead, the chamber of the spirit, water, and fire are used.

SECONDARY COMMENTARY

In cultivating the golden nectar of the sacred elixir, we must know which medicines are needed to build the foundations. Next we need to attend to the heating and cooling. The ascent of yang and the descent of yin correspond to the times of tzu and wu. The coming and going of the sun and moon occur at mao and yu. Use k'an and li to regulate the fire so that the dragon and tiger can become husband and wife. Return the essence of the sun to the empty hollow of the moon and cinnabar will form within the lead. Play with the Red Raven in the palace of li and mercury will emerge in the cinnabar. Gold is feeling and mercury is inner nature. When feeling and inner nature embrace, husband and wife are joined, and the golden nectar will naturally be created. Feeling and inner nature do not exist outside the human body. In the same manner, cinnabar and mercury live inside the lead. Like feelings and inner nature, cinnabar, mercury, and lead are a part of us. They are not unnatural substances.

Observe and understand the pattern of the rising and setting of the sun and the moon and the coming and going of yin and yang in the earth and the sky. The essences of ch'ien and k'un are often gathered in the mountains of the feet of the bird. The ancestor of the Great Medicine and the root of the Golden Elixir are deep inside the mysterious underworld.

The sun has three luminosities and the moon has three phases. When the sun and moon rise in the east, they illuminate the west. The true vapor of the best metal in the White Tiger of the west will enter the mysterious underworld and be transformed into the wu of the numeric six. When the sun and moon set in the west, they illuminate the east. The true vapor of the best wood of the Green Dragon in the east will enter the mysterious underworld and be transformed into the chi of the numeric six. When the sun and moon are in the center of the sky, they illuminate the north. The true vapor of the best fire of the Red Raven will enter the mysterious underworld. Earth will be created and transformed into black lead, which will dwell forever in the primal darkness as the root of all things. (See figure 9 for a summary of these relationships.)

The immortal Wei Po-yang says, "The sun hides its virtue and dulls its colors. The moon sends its virtue by giving light. When the sun is receptive and the moon nurtures, the body will not be injured." Know that the one true original vapor is the

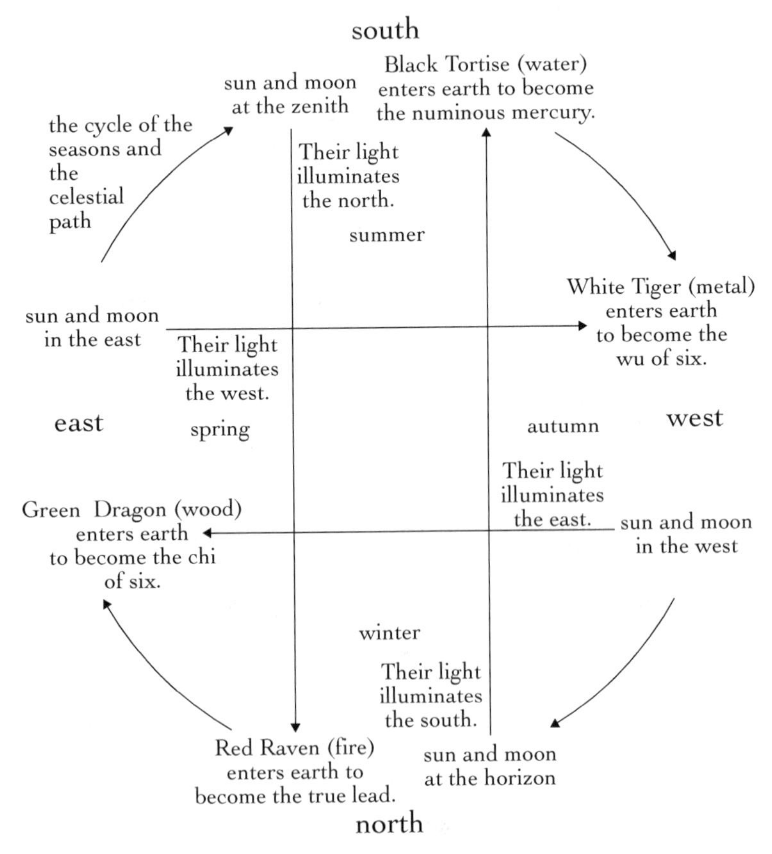

Figure 9. The positions of the sun and moon and their relationships to the creation of the alchemical catalysts (Red Raven and Black Tortoise) and the transformations of the alchemical ingredients (Green Dragon and White Tiger). The references to the Black Tortoise and the positions of the sun and moon are missing in the text and are reconstructed here.

creator of the earth and the sky. The wise ones of old understood that the sacred substance is hidden (in the sun and the moon). They formulated methods based on the pattern of changes and gathered the father and mother of the medicine. They patterned the chamber of the spirit after ch'ien and k'un and constructed the cauldron to resemble a bird's foot. They regulated the fire according to the cycles of the four seasons and returned metal and water to their origin. They did everything according to the principles of nature. They applied yang fire to return the essence to the sun and circulated yin fire to attract the soul of the moon. In this way, they directed the true vapor of the Three Domains back to the golden cauldron. They instilled supreme harmony into the four opposites and brought them together in the mysterious depths. Copulating in the undifferentiated chaos, they built the roots and foundations until the elixir was complete. Following the natural principles of change, they initiated the transformations.

Today many practitioners believe that quicksilver can be made into the Golden Elixir and ordinary lead can be used to drive the waterwheel. They mislead the future generations by confusing the false and the real. They try all kinds of techniques and achieve nothing at the end of their lives. They do not know that mercury is embodied in red cinnabar and that it emerges only when heat is applied. Mundane quicksilver can never be transformed into golden nectar. These practitioners do not know that the true golden nectar is made from the natural vapors of the sky and earth and the pure essences of yin and yang. Within the yin essence of the moon is the substance (red cinnabar) that is the ruler of yin. It resides in the Central Palace. Hidden in wu and chi, it is the father and mother of all medicines. How ridiculous it is to consider quicksilver and common metals found in the mountains and marshes as the father and mother of the sacred medicine! The sacred medicine is a treasure that can save the world and give us longevity. It is the ancestor of all things in the earth and sky, and it is not something easily recognizable by ordinary people. Practitioners today try to create the golden nectar with ordinary substances.

This is because they have misunderstood the teachings of the ancient sages. If the Golden Elixir could be made with mundane substances, then it would be very easy to produce it. The ancient sages spoke of lead and mercury symbolically, but people nowadays misunderstand the meaning. They take ordinary red cinnabar for the true lead and quicksilver for mercury. They mistake the false for the real and are confused about the nature of things. This is why they fail miserably in their search for longevity. What I have disclosed about how true lead is created is based on the classics passed down by the teachers. They are not words spoken casually to mislead future students. Let those who want to follow the Tao pay attention!

Translator's Note

The waterwheel is the Microcosmic Orbit, the circuit of energy that runs from the base of the spine up to the head, down through the palate of the mouth, and back to the tailbone.

3

Control Comes from the Ruler

Control comes from the ruler. The warrior puts down rebellions. The scholar exercises softness. The element earth flourishes in all four seasons. When the best earth is in command, it will take the sword to conquer adversities and protect the four directions.

Primary Commentary

Control comes from the ruler. The warrior puts down rebellions. The scholar exercises softness.

To control is to direct. The ruler issues commands to the forces in the four directions. The warrior is the fast hot fire. The scholar is the slow warm fire. When the golden cauldron is strong and firm, the chamber of the spirit is secure. In the beginning, initiate the warm fire in a clockwise direction to collect the harmonious yang vapor into the chamber of the cauldron. Apply fast fire in the final stage, and the golden nectar will flow out in a counterclockwise direction. The palace of k'un acts as a container. It keeps the essence inside, allowing the transformations to be completed. Like a ruler who is prepared to quell a rebellion before disorder breaks lose, we need to take the necessary precautions so that nothing can escape outside.

The element earth flourishes in all four seasons. When the best earth is in command, it will take the sword to conquer adversities and protect the four directions.

The best earth is the true earth of wu and chi. It is also the true lead. True lead can gather the vapor of harmony and return it to the Central Palace. If the vapors of the Green Dragon, White Tiger, Red Raven, and Black Tortoise are not nourished by the true earth, the golden nectar will never materialize. Earth occupies the Central Palace. Therefore it is called the supreme ruler. The vapor of harmony is born in the four seasons and is present in all things. The chamber of the spirit is the ruler of the vapor of harmony. It flourishes in all four seasons and can gather the essences of the sun and moon into the cauldron and prevent them from dissipating. The *Tsan-tung-chi* says, "Earth flourishes in the four seasons and permeates the beginning and the end."

Secondary Commentary

The supreme ruler is the one who governs the world. Internally, he promotes virtue and culture. Externally, he exercises military caution. His laws are based on those of the Three Kings. The hundred provinces of his kingdom are provided for. The five grains are planted in accordance with the seasons. The country is peaceful and prosperous and the vapor of harmony flourishes. The ancient ones patterned their methods of creating the golden nectar of the sacred elixir on the principles of governing a country. First they built the chamber of the spirit. Next they enclosed the fetus in the chamber of the spirit. Then they surrounded the fetus with the golden cauldron. Outside the golden cauldron they placed the hearth. Each item was prepared meticulously so that the essence of the golden nectar could grow.

The vapor of supreme harmony brings things together. The ruler is the sacred mother in the Central Palace of the body. It holds the liquid pearl and prevents it from flying away. The slow warm fire is used to initiate the process and the fast hot fire is used to complete it. It is in this way that the golden nectar is created. After Kung-sen successfully ascended to the immortal realm, we knew that the vapor of harmony comes from the best earth. It permeates the four seasons, embraces metal and water, harmonizes the liquid pearl, and is gradually transformed into the sacred medicine. The liquid pearl is a beautiful woman. It is elusive and does not stay in one place. Only the element earth can contain it and transform it. This is all part of the natural way of things.

Translator's Notes

The golden nectar, which is the Golden Elixir of Immortality, flows in a counterclockwise direction. Its direction of flow should not be confused with the direction of movement of the yang fire (which is clockwise) and the yin fire (which is counterclockwise). The direction of flow of the golden nectar is said to be counterclockwise because the energy is directed back into the body. This is contrasted with the flow of mundane energy, which is clockwise, because mundane energy flows out of the body.

Wu and chi are celestial stems. Refer to the introduction for a discussion of their roles in the alchemical process. Also refer to the caption of figure 1 for a clarification between the wu of the celestial stem and the wu of the terrestrial branch.

The Three Kings were legendary rulers in ancient China.

4

The Numerics of K'an and Li Are One and Two

The numerics of k'an and li are one and two. They move exclusively between north and south. They occupy the highest place among the seventy-two minerals.

Primary Commentary

The numerics of k'an and li are one and two.

The numeric one of sky gives birth to water in k'an. Therefore water is governed by the numeric one. The numeric two of earth gives birth to fire in li. Therefore fire is governed by the numeric two.

They move exclusively between north and south.

North is where yin reaches its zenith. It is also where the vapor of yang first appears. Passing through tzu, ch'ou, yin, mao, ch'en, and ssu, it ends at the palace of the trigram sun. South is where yang reaches its zenith. It is also where the vapor of yin first appears. Passing through wu, wei, shen, yu, hsü, and hai, it ends at the palace of the trigram ch'ien. The vapors of yin and yang emerge and disappear in wu and tzu. Therefore it is said that they move exclusively between north and south.

They occupy the highest place among the seventy-two minerals.

The vapor of the true lead was there before sky and earth came into existence. Its form, however, materialized only after sky and earth were separated. Therefore it occupies the highest position in the order of things and is the foundation of the elixir.

Secondary Commentary

Today human efforts that are called "the secret and mysterious arts" are primarily involved with heating ordinary gold and refining silver to obtain the so-called treasures. These efforts have all come to nothing. Even if something is produced, the product is neither a rare treasure nor something that can prolong life or help humanity.

Practitioners nowadays do not know that life and inner nature are of utmost importance. They delude each other and do not understand the true principles. They do not know that the key to the Great Elixir and the production of the medicine lies in the interaction of the yin and yang energies. The alchemical treatises written by the immortals say, "In refining the treasures, one needs to be united with the subtle. In refining the subtle, one needs to be united with the numinous spirit. In refining the numinous spirit, one needs to be united with the sacred spirit. In refining the sacred spirit, one needs to be united with the Tao." These statements tell us how to distinguish a real elixir from a false one. They also show us the difference between a superficial and a deep understanding of the subtle principles. If you do not encounter the secret instructions of the enlightened ones, how can you know the complete truth and be liberated from the dust of the world?

The trigrams k'an and li symbolize water and fire. South and north are the locations where fire and water originate. Although fire and water have different qualities, the two come from the same origin. When divided, they have different properties. When united, their forms disappear and they become one. The enlightened ones knew that all these things are part of the natural order. They also knew that the union cannot be artificially engineered. Therefore they were able to compound the two substances and produce the highest treasure. Ingest this thing and you will attain longevity. The sky created two substances. These substances are the essences of the sun and moon and the bone and marrow of ch'ien and k'un. The *I Ching* says, "The sky gave us two phenomena and the sages made use of them."

The path of returning to the origin begins with action and ends with nonaction. Water and fire, k'an and li, rise and fall between south and north. Therefore, in the making of the elixir, they occupy the highest positions among the seventy-two minerals. If you know the principles of creation and dissolution in nature and understand the cycles of movement of the sun and moon, you will know the true nature of existence and nonexistence.

Translator's Notes

In Taoist cosmology, the five elements—water, fire, wood, metal, and earth—are each associated with a pair of numbers. Water is associated with the numbers one and six, fire with two and seven, wood with three and eight, metal with four and nine, and earth with five and ten. These are the numerics of precreation. They describe the original state of things before creation. Sky and earth are the agents of creation. Sky is associated with odd numbers and earth with even numbers. Odd numbers represent the power of initiation necessary to start life. Even numbers represent the power of nourishment necessary to complete life. Thus, when sky and earth created the elements, the numeric one of sky generated water and the numeric six of earth completed it. The numeric seven of sky generated fire and the numeric two of earth completed it. The author of the Primary Commentary assumed that readers were familiar with Taoist cosmology; therefore the functions of the odd and even numerics in creation were not described completely and were simply referred to as "the numeric one giving birth to water and the numeric two giving birth to fire."

Note that in the Primary Commentary, the author is discussing the waxing and waning of the yang and yin fires in the twelve segments of the day (see figures 5 and 7).

5

Hardness and Softness Embrace

Hardness and softness embrace. Yin and yang follow their natural tendencies. Metal and fire perform their duties. Metal and water accept each other. Female and male become one. Everything functions in an orderly way.

PRIMARY COMMENTARY

Hardness and softness embrace. Yin and yang follow their natural tendencies.

The yang of ch'ien is hard. The yin of k'un is soft. When they embrace, the chamber of the spirit will emerge. This allows the natural vapors of yin and yang and the essences of the sun and moon to be gathered into the golden womb to make the elixir. Thus the *Tsan-tung-chi* says, "The hardness of ch'ien and the softness of k'un embrace and copulate."

Metal and fire perform their functions. Metal and water accept each other.

Externally, water and fire strengthen each other. Internally, metal and water copulate. The wood of mercury gives birth to the body of the Green Dragon, and the essence of metal nourishes the fetus of the White Tiger. The bright sprouts bloom, but metal and wood retain their form. After metal and water have copulated in the chamber of the spirit for a period of time, the sacred water will be born inside the mother's womb and the elixir will emerge. Mother and child hold on to each other in tenderness and are nourished by metal and water.

Female and male become one. Everything functions in an orderly way.

Female and male are the Green Dragon and the White Tiger respectively. They are also the moon and the sun, yin and yang, k'an and li, wife and husband, water and fire, and woman and man. When female and male copulate, generative energy and vapor are produced. If everything functions properly, the desired results will occur naturally.

Secondary Commentary

Male is associated with the trigram li, the symbol of the Great Yang of the sun. Female is associated with the trigram k'an, the symbol of the Great Yin of the moon. When sun and moon copulate, metal and water are created. Feeling and inner nature accept each other because they are a natural pair. No other ingredients are needed. Using ordinary substances to create the sacred medicine would go against the natural way.

When a young male reaches puberty and a young female becomes sexually productive, feelings of attraction will develop between them. This is part of the natural order of things. Therefore it is not surprising that the ancient sages compared the making of the Great Elixir to human procreation. Cinnabar and mercury lie in the body of lead. They emerge when lead is excited by water and fire. Therefore they are not external substances. The fetus in the womb is created by the interaction of water and fire. It is also a substance in the body. The ancient people knew that these substances are like feeling and inner nature. Neither can exist without the other. Therefore they collected the essences of the dragon and the tiger and circulated the vapors of metal and water to produce the supreme medicine.

The Tao consists of yin and yang. If this were not a part of the natural order of things, the two would not exist together. For example, when male and female copulate, the procreative energies will interact and transformations will occur. The human fetus is not produced by external substances. Similarly, the sacred medicine, which is made from li and k'an, does not contain substances foreign to the body. Refining the true essences of the sun and moon to produce the golden nectar is like creating the human fetus in the sexual union of man and woman. The only difference is that the former is the way of the immortals and the latter is the way of mortals. The enlightened ones used this analogy because they feared that future students would not understand the true meaning (of the Golden Elixir). As for the meaning of the other symbols, you should be able to deduce them yourselves.

6

The Transformation of the Spirit Is Patterned after the Hexagrams Chi and Wei

The transformation of the spirit is patterned after the hexagrams chi and wei. Reaching the end, the process returns to the beginning. The period is marked by the ninth day of the lunar month, when yang becomes harmonious in the morning and evening. Having completed its circuit, yang is united with the celestial mind. The yang components of the hexagram end at ssu. Pure yin emerges at li and wu. It passes through the southern position of ting and ends at the hour of hai.

Primary Commentary

The transformation of the spirit is patterned after the hexagrams chi and wei. Reaching the end, the process returns to the beginning.

The Great Elixir must be incubated for one month. If the amount of fire is applied incorrectly or if the cauldron is not sealed, the spirit energy will be low and the golden nectar will not crystallize in time. Therefore it is said that the elixir must be completed within one month. The *Tsan-tung-chi* says, "Reaching the time of wei and passing from new moon to another new moon—this is what is meant by returning to the beginning."

The period is marked by the ninth day of the lunar month, when yang becomes harmonious in the morning and evening.

During the hour of tzu on the night of the last day of the darkest moon, yang fire begins to glow. It is symbolized by the earth-thunder hexagram of fu. The yang component in the hexagram is born in k'un. On the ninth day it is at the bottom of the hexagram. The hours between tzu and ssu are referred to as morning or day, and the hours between wu and hai are referred to as evening or night. The hexagram tun rules the hours of the morning and the hexagram mong rules the hours of the evening. Thus the hexagrams tun and mong govern the twelve segments of the day, their behavior corresponding to that of the Great Elixir. Two hexagrams govern each day. Therefore there are sixty governing hexagrams per month. Tun and mong rule the beginning, and wei and chi rule the end. This is what the *Tsan-tung-chi* means when it says, "The dawning of the day marks the period, and movement and stillness have their mornings and evenings."

Having completed its circuit, yang is united with the celestial mind. The yang components of the hexagram end at ssu.

Yang fire begins at tzu and reaches its height at ssu. At wu, yin is born. This is what the *Tsan-tung-chi* means when it says, "Spring and summer reside in the body. It is the period from tzu through ch'en to ssu."

Pure yin emerges at li and wu. It passes through the southern position of ting and ends at the hour of hai.

Yin fire arrives at wu and is strongest at hai. At tzu, yang fire is born again. This is what the *Tsan-tung-chi* means when it says,

"Externally, apply autumn and winter. It is the period from wu through hsü to hai."

Secondary Commentary

The transformations of the Great Elixir begin with the hexagrams ch'ien and k'un. Yang fire starts at tzu and yin fire starts at wu. The yang of ch'ien reaches its height at ssu and the yin of k'un is strongest at hai. The twelve yin and yang components of ch'ien and k'un change according to the twelve segments of the day.

The Great Elixir will not materialize if you just sit around and wait. If you are not clear about the principles, you will waste your effort and resources. Your body will become old and tired and nothing will be accomplished. Know that the Tao embraces the sky and earth. It exhales and inhales yin and yang. It moves the four seasons and rotates the sun and moon. It circulates day and night and creates and nourishes all things. These transformations occur naturally because they are a part of the Tao. The enlightened ones knew that the root of the Tao can help humanity. They observed its laws in the sky and the earth and were in harmony with yin and yang. They gathered the spirit of the sun and the soul of the moon and compounded them with the numinous vapors of water and fire to produce the supreme medicine. In this manner, they returned to the natural way. They recorded their teachings in treatises to benefit the future generations. However, many practitioners today do not believe the ancient wisdom and think that they can mimic creation by compounding ordinary substances. To the end, they lose sight of the supreme principles. Even if a product is created, it cannot return youth to the aged or bestow longevity to the living. Worse still, the concoctions may cause poisoning and internal bleeding if ingested. Those who cultivate the elixir should be aware of these things.

Translator's Note

The pair of hexagrams wei and chi are wei-ch'i and chi-ch'i respectively. These two hexagrams consist of the trigrams k'an and li and they symbolize the balance or harmony of water and fire. A discussion of the special events in the firing process and an explanation of these hexagrams can be found in the introduction.

7

Water and Fire Have Their Own Territory

Water and fire have their own territory. They keep to their domain, becoming winter and summer. Benevolence and integrity are manifested in the east and west. The five elements govern the cycle of the four seasons. In this way, yin and yang make use of each other. Following the numerics of one and three, everything is kept in order.

PRIMARY COMMENTARY

Water and fire have their own territory. They keep to their domain, becoming winter and summer.

Water is yin and is coldest in k'an. Fire is yang and is hottest in li. Each remains in its own territory to become winter and summer. The *Tsan-tung-chi* says, "Reward and punishment are given in spring and autumn, and dimness and brightness follow the paths of winter and summer."

Benevolence and integrity are manifested in the east and west. The five elements govern the cycle of the four seasons.

East is associated with the element wood. It is where all things begin their growth. Therefore it is identified with benevolence and joy. West is associated with the element metal. It is where things die. Therefore it is identified with integrity and anger. The vapors of metal, wood, water, fire, and earth govern the changes in the four seasons and determine the weather. This is what the *Tsan-tung-chi* means when it says, "The hexagrams display benevolence and integrity and can erupt spontaneously in joy or anger."

In this way, yin and yang make use of each other. Following the numerics of one and three, everything is kept in order.

If the numerics of the four directions do not deviate from their natural sequence, the vapors of yin and yang will flow smoothly, and water and fire, winter and summer, will keep to their course.

Secondary Commentary

The movement of the sun and moon and the passing of winter and summer follow orderly cycles. When the sun disappears, the moon appears. When one year ends, the next year arrives. The energy of the year permeates the twelve segments of each day and orders spring, summer, autumn, and winter according to the laws of the four seasons. The behaviors of all natural phenomena are therefore orderly. The sun and the moon travel their celestial paths. Winter and summer come on time. It is in this manner that the Great Elixir is created. Everything is patterned after the natural laws, and that which is inside must know what is happening outside. When yin and yang are united in the cauldron, generative energy and vapor will emerge in the chamber. Receiving the generative energy and vapor of yin and yang, the interior of the cauldron becomes moist and shiny. When circulation is smooth and natural, the transformations will gradually occur, following the sequence of the four seasons.

The five treatises write, "Spring gives warmth and is like benevolence. Summer gives heat and is like propriety. Autumn brings coolness and is like integrity. Winter is cold and is like intelligence." If the four seasons follow the natural cycle, all endeavors will be successful throughout the year. The vapor of spring gives life to all things. It is the yang fire that occurs before ssu. The vapor of autumn takes away the life of all things. It is the yin fire that occurs after wu. Tzu, ch'ou, and yin are spring. Mao, ch'en, and ssu are summer. Wu, wei, and shen are autumn. Yu, hsü, and hai are winter. They determine the firing process in the twelve segments of the day. The process must correspond to the cycles of the four seasons and the five elements. If everything is done correctly, something will materialize inside the cauldron. The golden nectar will be gathered and the elixir will be completed. There is a poem that says, "The sages had the key to the principles of transformation. They plucked the sun and moon and placed them inside the furnace. Softly and subtly they stirred the essences of the sky and earth. Wielding yin and yang, they chased away the spirits and ghosts." However, if the laws of the sky and earth are not followed, if yin and yang are not applied correctly, and if the transformations are unnatural, the golden nectar of the sacred elixir will never materialize.

8

Set Up Positions in the Chamber of the Spirit

Set up positions in the chamber of the spirit and the transformations will occur within. The chamber of the spirit consists of an upper and a lower crucible. Establishing the positions means intertwining the female and male. In the transformation, cinnabar and mercury emerge. In the creation of cinnabar and mercury, metal and earth are applied. The application of these two substances is not tied to the positions of the yin and yang components in the trigrams. The winged one flies to the precarious void. Cinnabar and mercury are elusive in their coming and going. The positions of the upper and lower crucibles are also unstable. The only thing that is certain is that cinnabar and mercury dissolve when they return to the Central Palace. Only earth can control cinnabar and mercury, for earth embodies the essence of all the minerals and is the ancestor of the elixir.

Primary Commentary

Set up positions in the chamber of the spirit and the transformations will occur within.

The chamber of the spirit is patterned after the sky and the earth. When the positions of sky and earth are established, the light of the sun and moon will shine. This is what the *Tsan-tung-chi* means when it says, "When sky and earth establish their positions, changes will occur within."

The chamber of the spirit consists of an upper and a lower crucible.

The chamber of the spirit consists of an upper and a lower crucible because it is patterned after sky and earth. The *Tsan-tung-chi* says, "Sky and earth refer to ch'ien and k'un."

Establishing the positions means intertwining the female and male.

This means establishing the positions of sky and earth and ch'ien and k'un. The upper crucible is patterned after the sky. It is male and ch'ien. The lower crucible is patterned after the earth. It is female and k'un. The upper and lower crucibles are joined to become one structure. The *Tsan-tung-chi* says, "To set up the positions is to let the yin and yang be coupled."

In the transformation, cinnabar and mercury emerge. In the creation of cinnabar and mercury, metal and earth are applied.

Set up the cauldron according to the laws of ch'ien and k'un. Put the mother of metal in the center and equip the Three Domains. The numinous mercury will then emerge. Cinnabar and mercury are the water of k'an and the fire of li. They are ch'ien and k'un applied. The *Tsan-tung-chi* says, "Change comes from k'an and li. They are ch'ien and k'un applied."

The application of these two substances is not tied to the positions of the yin and yang components in the trigrams. The winged one flies to the precarious void.

Ch'ien and k'un are the sun and the moon. The ascent and descent of the sun and moon and the regulation of water and fire are not tied to the yin and yang components in the trigrams. The winged one is the fire of li in the south. The precarious void is the water of k'an in the north. This is what the *Tsan-tung-chi* means when it says, "The two applications are not tied to the yin and yang components of the trigrams. They flow and wander around in the six voids."

Cinnabar and mercury are elusive in their coming and going. The positions of the upper and lower crucibles are also unstable.

The coming and going of water and fire in the chamber of the spirit are not confined to particular areas. This is what the *Tsan-tung-chi* means when it says, "The coming and going cannot be predicted and the positions of the upper and lower crucibles also fluctuate."

The only thing that is certain is that cinnabar and mercury dissolve when they return to the Central Palace.

If fire is regulated properly, the substances will continuously be dissolved into the Central Palace to become the golden nectar. The *Tsan-tung-chi* says, "Resting in the depths, hidden in the fallen, it ascends and descends at the center."

Only earth can control cinnabar and mercury, for earth embodies the essence of all the minerals and is the ancestor of the elixir.

The chamber of the spirit in the Central Palace is made of true lead. Therefore it is called the best earth. It contains the essence of all minerals and is the ancestor of the golden nectar. The *Tsan-tung-chi* says, "It embraces all things and is the ancestor of the elixir."

Secondary Commentary

The key to the Great Elixir lies in silver and lead, and cinnabar and mercury. Cinnabar and mercury are the essence of the sun, and silver and lead are the essence of the moon. The formula for cultivating the golden nectar is found in the subtle patterns of the sky and the earth. This should be clear from the previous chapters. In case future generations of students do not understand, the principles are explained again here. If everything is understood clearly, cinnabar and mercury can be obtained without any effort. Lead is attracted to cinnabar and mercury the way two people are pulled together by feelings of love. Feelings originate inside and are directed outside. Similarly, cinnabar and mercury are born internally and manifested externally. Just as feeling and inner nature are a part of a human being, lead and mercury are not external to the body. Cinnabar and mercury are hidden within the lead. When feelings are aroused, they are directed outside. Cinnabar and mercury both grow inside lead. Make sure that these substances are used well. All principles are the same. It is the intention of the enlightened ones to teach us how to combine the supreme essences of the sun and the moon to create the medicine. Do not rely on substances that are not a part of us.

Translator's Notes

The six voids are the six spaces of the hexagrams where the yin (broken lines) and yang (solid lines) are located.

Recall from the introduction that in the firing process, the circulation of yang fire is symbolized by the trigrams chen, tui, and ch'ien and the circulation of yin fire is symbolized by the trigrams sun, ken, and k'un. K'an and li are not part of the scheme of trigrams describing the waxing and waning of the yin and yang fires. Therefore it is said that they are not tied to the yin and yang components of the trigrams.

9

Substance and Nonsubstance Control Each Other

Substance and nonsubstance control each other. The Red Raven flies in the sky. Purple rays illuminate the sun. Cinnabar and mercury both dissolve.

PRIMARY COMMENTARY

Substance and nonsubstance control each other. The Red Raven flies in the sky.

The tiger is substance and the dragon is nonsubstance. Also, white metal has substance and the vapors of yin and yang are nonsubstantive. If we use only white metal to build the chamber of the spirit, the transformations will not occur. However, when the rise and fall of water and fire are matched with the four seasons, the elixir will be created. Therefore it is said that the empty vessel is used to control and hold the substances. The Red Raven is the descending vapor of the sacred fire. Within the chamber of the spirit, golden nectar is created in the fire. This is what the *Tsan-tung-chi* means when it says, "Nonsubstance is used to support the substance. Using the vessel means applying emptiness."

Purple rays illuminate the sun. Cinnabar and mercury both dissolve.

The purple rays are the supreme essence of the sun. Inside the sacred cauldron, they are transformed into the golden aura of the light of the sun and the moon. Sometimes they are also transformed into the numinous nectar and appear as a dragon and a tiger. Glowing within the cauldron, they become cinnabar and mercury. Waxing and waning, floating and sinking, their creation and dissolution follow the movement of water and fire. This is what the *Tsan-tung-chi* means when it says, "Waxing and waning, k'an and li are extinguished."

Secondary Commentary

In the ancient times, people used only quicksilver to make the elixir. They needed the dragon but not the tiger. They did not have to pattern themselves after the five elements and the four seasons. Nor did they need to devise methods based on the natural laws of the sky and the earth. They did not have to gather the yang and yin of husband and wife and intertwine the male and female. They simply took the vapors of yin and yang in k'an and li and let them wax and wane inside the body. They let the essences of the dragon and the tiger penetrate and nourish the seven cavities. They trusted the process to nature and allowed things to follow the great way of the Tao. Therefore, in the ancient times, people lived a long life and did not die unnaturally.

In our era, if people want to return to their youth, lengthen their life span, and rise to the subtle realm of immortality, they will need to build the furnace and set up the cauldron. They will also need to gather the vapor of supreme harmony from the sky and the earth and recover the numinous essences of the sun and the moon. The four families must be complete and the five elements must be ready. After nine circulations and three thousand hours, a purple powder will materialize inside the cauldron. The golden aura emanating from it will rival the bright sun. Ingest it and you will attain longevity and age with the sky and the earth.

Nowadays many people recognize the tiger but few know about the dragon. The golden nectar is the sun and the ancestor of the best wood in the Green Dragon of the east. The yellow sprout is the moon and the ancestor of the golden nectar of the White Tiger of the west. The essences of these two substances have the power of transformation. Therefore the classics say, "The essences of the sun and moon can help the old and weak." If you follow the correct methods, the transformations will occur within. The transformation involves cinnabar becoming quicksilver, which is the yang returning to yin, and quicksilver becoming cinnabar, which is the yin returning to yang. This elixir is called the elixir of pure yang because if people ingest it, they will attain longevity. The sages used metaphors to tell us that other than the spirit of the sun in k'an and the soul of the moon in li, no other substances are involved in the making of the elixir. This information is stated explicitly so that future students will not be confused.

10

Instructions Are Not Given Superfluously

Instructions are not given superfluously and theories are not just empty talk. The words in the texts reveal the mysteries and unlock the numinous. The information is displayed in the yin and yang components of the hexagrams. The path lies in the cycle of the five elements. The male in k'an is the essence of metal. The female in li is the light of the fire. Metal and wood control each other. Water and fire subdue each other. Earth grows strong in the home of metal. The three substances are dissolved. When the four seas are gathered, there will be peace and balance. All this is accomplished by the emperor of the wood in the Central Palace.

Primary Commentary

Instructions are not given superfluously and theories are not just empty talk.

The sages did not present false information when they wrote down their teachings. Nor did they intend to confuse the future generations. The *Tsan-tung-chi* says, "The words are not made up casually and the principles do not materialize from thin air."

The words in the texts reveal the mysteries and unlock the numinous.

Excessive explanations are avoided and the key points are emphasized to reveal the subtle laws of the sun and moon and penetrate the essence of the numinous. This is what the *Tsan-tung-chi* means when it says, "Observe and examine the effects to learn about the numinous."

The information is displayed in the yin and yang components of the hexagrams. The path lies in the cycle of the five elements.

The numerics of firing are patterned after the sixty-four hexagrams of the *Chou-i (I Ching)*. Waxing and waning follow the cycle of the five elements of metal, wood, water, fire, and earth. The union of the sun and moon is likened to the relationship of husband and wife. The copulation of k'an and li is used to describe how the supreme essence is gathered. This is what the *Tsan-tung-chi* means when it says, "The nature of things can be deduced from the words, and the original principles can be intuited from the examples."

The male in k'an is the essence of metal. The female in li is the light of the fire.

The numeric six of wu is hidden in k'an and it is the essence of the moon. It is where the yang of the male is located and it is positioned in the north. The moon is yin, and wu is yang. Therefore wu is the yang within the yin. It symbolizes the birth of the metal tiger in water. The numeric six of chi is hidden in li and it is the light of the sun. It is where the yin of the female is located and it is positioned in the south. The sun is yang, and chi is yin. Therefore chi is the yin within the yang. It symbolizes the birth of the mercuric dragon in the fire. This is what the *Tsan-tung-chi* means when it says, "K'an and wu are the essence of the moon; li and chi are the light of the sun."

Metal and wood control each other. Water and fire subdue each other.

Metal is white metal and wood is red mercury. When these two substances control each other, their strength is increased.

When water and fire subdue each other, a bright light will be revealed. When the sun and moon copulate and hardness and softness excite each other, yin and yang will unite according to the natural laws. The *Tsan-tung-chi* says, "When changes follow the behavior of the sun and moon, hardness and softness will unite."

Earth grows strong in the home of metal. The three substances are dissolved.

The three elements metal, wood, and fire are immersed in the last fires of the four seasons. After nine cycles of circulation, they dissolve into bright dust. The *Tsan-tung-chi* says, "Earth waxes in all four seasons and penetrates the beginning and the end."

When the four seas are gathered, there will be peace and balance.

Breathe in the vapor of the four directions and return them to the sacred cauldron. Gather the essences of the dragon and the tiger and make them into the supreme medicine. Use the numeric five of the element earth to complete the process. Use the four seasons to contain it. Let red, green, black, and white perform their functions. The sacred elixir will then be completed. This is what the *Tsan-tung-chi* means when it says, "Green, red, black, and white each reside in their own position."

All this is accomplished by the emperor of the wood in the Central Palace.

The best wood in the Central Palace is the vapor of supreme harmony of wu and chi. The principles that direct the transformation of the golden elixir are based on wu and chi. Since wu and chi reside in the Central Palace, they are given the name "emperor." People who cultivate the sacred elixir gather the essences of the sun and moon and combine them with the numinous vapor of yin and yang. When the cycle of the celestial circulation is complete, water and fire will have finished their course. All this is accomplished by the emperor of the best wood. This is what the *Tsan-tung-chi* means when it says, "What happens in the Central Palace is the work of the emperor of the best wood."

Secondary Commentary

The ancients do not speak unless it is necessary, and they do not like to repeat instructions. After they had succeeded in their endeavors, they recorded the teachings in the *Tsan-tung-chi* to guide future seekers of the Tao. However, their writings only discuss general ideas. In this commentary, I have decided to reveal the origin of the Great Medicine so that future generations will not be deluded into using substances like ordinary cinnabar and quicksilver. If you understand the mysterious and subtle principles and follow the movements of the sky and earth, yin and yang, and the four seasons, you will attain the elixir. This is because you are using the true yin and true yang. The *Yin-fu ching* (The Yin Convergence Classic) states, "When the celestial ways are revealed, you will not die. Those who have attained this knowledge should not transmit it to dishonest people." The *Tsan-tung-chi* says, "When too much is written, it is feared that the celestial way will be betrayed. This is why I hesitate about writing all this down."

The cultivation of the supreme medicine does not require anything other than water and fire. When water and fire copulate, the energies of the dragon and the tiger will unite in the cauldron to become the golden nectar. True lead is the father and mother of the Golden Elixir. The numinous mercury is its ancestor. They created all things and nourished all life. If you can anchor the body with the true lead and know the true locations of water and fire, how can you not succeed in making the Great Elixir?

Translator's Note

Red is associated with south, black with north, green with east, and white with west. Notice that these are the colors of the four animals—Red Raven, Black Tortoise, Green Dragon, White Tiger. For a discussion of the numerics of the five elements, you can refer to the translator's notes in chapter 4.

11

The Fire of Metal Is the True Lead

The fire of metal is the true lead. The glow in the cinnabar powder comes from metal and fire. The subtleties of transformation have been discussed in detail elsewhere. When yang stirs, yin wanes. The undifferentiated whole emerges when the numerics of one and nine are complete. The precious essence now coalesces. The medicine corresponds to the pattern of the hexagrams. Metal has 384 pearls. They weigh one pound, or sixteen ounces. When the essence of metal melts, the two vapors (yin and yang) become the elixir. At the appointed time, fire is applied to the Green Dragon. The chamber of the spirit refines the essence. Metal and fire mutually push and pump. The yang of the male nourishes the mysterious water. The yin of the female turns the red into gold. Yin and yang intertwine in copulation. The liquid essence embraces the primordial vapor. All things are created from the void and are nurtured to become their kind. Of all the elixirs, this one is the most numinous. It is the source of longevity.

Primary Commentary

The fire of metal is the true lead.

Metal and fire are the essences of the sun and moon. Metal is the inner nature of the moon and fire is the root of the sun.

Both are born inside the lead. For immortal Wei Po-yang, metal and fire represent change, and change is medicine. The *Tsan-tung-chi* states that "change means pattern."

The glow in the cinnabar powder comes from metal and fire.

The cinnabar powder is the golden nectar. The golden nectar is but one type of elixir. It is made from the essences of the sun and moon. Metal is lead, moon is water, cinnabar is mercury, and the sun is fire. Externally, water and fire ascend and descend. Internally, lead and mercury copulate. Other than this, there is nothing else. The transformation of the golden cinnabar is made possible by the essences of the sun and moon. This is what the *Tsan-tung-chi* means when it says, "Hanging high, it is bright. It is none other than the sun and moon."

The subtleties of transformation have been discussed in detail elsewhere. When yang stirs, yin wanes.

The ancients have penetrated the subtleties and observed the waxing and waning of things. Thus they were able to let the vapors of yin and yang come and go, stir and settle, circulate night and day, and cycle endlessly. This is what the *Tsan-tung-chi* means when it says, "Exhaust the sacred to know the transformations. When yang departs, yin arrives."

The undifferentiated whole emerges when the numerics of one and nine are complete. The precious essence now coalesces.

The vapors of k'an and li and the energies of the dragon and the tiger are mixed in the chamber of the spirit to wax and wane with the fire. In the beginning of the process, fire is initiated in the palace of the numeric one in the position of k'an. Essence and vapor interact, but the transformation is not complete. When it reaches ssu and shen, the fire becomes hot, and the dragon gives birth to mercury and the tiger gives birth to lead. The essences of lead and mercury begin to glow, and the vapors of the sun and moon in the cauldron will be manifested outside. Simultaneously, the essences of water and fire are inserted smoothly inside. The *Tsan-tung-chi* says, "Gathering momentum like a turning wheel, the entering and exiting are smooth."

The medicine corresponds to the pattern of the hexagrams. Metal has 384 pearls. They weigh one pound, or sixteen ounces.

There are 384 components in the hexagrams. They match the numerics of the celestial cycle of the year and govern the firing process of one circulation. Metal has 384 pearls. The numeric of the mother of metal matches one pound and is sufficient to make one pound of the Great Elixir. The firing process corresponds to the mother of metal. This is what the *Tsan-tung-chi* means when it says, "There are 384 components of change. They correspond to the application of fire."

When the essence of metal melts, the two vapors (yin and yang) become the elixir. At the appointed time, fire is applied to the Green Dragon.

The Great Yin is the nectar of the metal tiger. The Great Yang is the saliva of the wood dragon. Both are transformed to become the true elixir. The fires begin at the new moon. They are ruled by the fire spirit of the Green Dragon and are governed by the hexagram chen. The *Tsan-tung-chi* says, "With the birth of the new moon, the hexagram chen comes to apply the fire."

At the appointed time, fire is applied to the Green Dragon. The chamber of the spirit refines the essence. Metal and fire mutually push and pump.

When the Green Dragon is stimulated by fire, the vapors of the dragon and tiger will intertwine inside the chamber of the spirit. As metal and fire copulate, they will be transformed into the sacred elixir. This is what the *Tsan-tung-chi* means when it says, "At the appointed time, sky and earth exchange their essences and the sun and moon embrace in a tryst."

The yang of the male nourishes the mysterious water. The yin of the female turns the red into gold.

Male is yang. It is ch'ien, sky, ancient yang, the sun, and cinnabar. Its essence is the mysterious water or mercury. Female is yin. It is k'un, earth, ancient yin, the moon, and lead. Its essence is the yellow gold or white gold. When the sun and moon copulate in the cauldron, the sun is transformed into the mysterious water and the moon is transformed into yellow gold. The yellow gold is lead and the mysterious water is the true mercury. When lead and mercury are coupled to become one, the elixir emerges. The *Tsan-tung-chi* says, "The yang of the male swirls and emits the mysterious water. The yin of the female is transformed into the yellow cocoon."

Yin and yang intertwine in copulation. The liquid essence embraces the primordial vapor.

The vapors of yin and yang and the dragon and tiger transform each other when water and fire interact, generating the saliva and nectar, which are the foundations of the elixir. The *Tsan-tung-chi* says, "Copulating in the undifferentiated chaos, power is sent down through the roots of the tree."

All things are created from the void and are nurtured to become their kind.

All things in the world receive life from the primordial vapor. Once they are formed, they will become what they are. For example, in the cauldron the vapor of wood becomes the dragon, while the vapor of metal becomes the tiger. The vapor of fire is transformed into mercury, the vapor of water is transformed into lead, and the vapor of earth becomes the agent of harmony. The five vapors return to the Central Palace to cultivate the roots and foundations so that the spirit can become immortal. These things occur naturally because it is the way things are made. The *Tsan-tung-chi* says, "Work diligently to cultivate the roots and foundations. Gather the spirit to complete the form."

Of all the elixirs, this one is the most numinous. It is the source of longevity.

There are twenty-four kinds of golden nectar. The one discussed here is the supreme golden nectar of the Great Elixir. It is the path that leads to ascending the sky in bright daylight. Its making is patterned in detail after the sky and the earth. The sun, the moon, the stars, the five elements, and the four seasons are all returned to the chamber of the spirit to be transformed into the golden nectar. All methods of longevity start from here. The *Tsan-tung-chi* says, "Everyone jumps out from here. This is where the worm emerges."

Secondary Commentary

The fire of metal is the fire of lead. The fire of lead is the fire of water. When metal and fire interact, cinnabar powder will emerge within the true lead. The ancients kept the knowledge of the firing process secret. If the numeric of fire measures one pound, the base numeric is one pound. The base amount of one pound is divided into 384 pearls. The measure of one pound of fire is divided into 384 components of change. This matches with the movement of the sixty-four hexagrams in the year. Thus the process in ch'ien consists of 216 and the process of k'un consists of 144 components of change. Expanding these principles, we can understand how all things are nourished. The numerics of ten thousand are 1,520. This corresponds to the numerics of the ten thousand myriad things and matches one cycle of movement of the sky and the earth. The ancient ones knew the laws of the sky and the earth and predicted the movement of yin and yang. They applied the flow and ebb of water and fire to metal and wood. Integrating hardness and softness, they mastered the way of creation.

The hexagrams ch'ien and k'un reveal the numerics of the

firing process of the Great Elixir. The subtleties of metal, wood, water, fire, and earth are patterned after phenomena in the sky. The cultivation of the supreme medicine and the circulation of fire match the numerics of celestial movement. The numerics of the year, month, and day are applied to the twelve segments of the day. This schedule is then used to regulate the waxing and waning of the yin and yang fires to cultivate the golden nectar of the sacred elixir. When everything is done correctly, you will attain the principles of creation.

Translator's Note

Here the numerics of one and nine refer to water and fire respectively. These are post-creation numerics and should not be confused with the pre-creation numerics described in chapter 4. Post-creation numerics can be activated by human effort, while pre-creation numerics are not subject to human control. In post-creation numerics, water is associated with the number one, fire with nine, wood with three and four, metal with six and seven, and earth with two, five, and eight. The post-creation numerics of one (water) and nine (fire) refer to the circulation of the yin and yang fires in the production of the Golden Elixir.

12

It Becomes Subtle and Moist, Bright and Shiny

It becomes subtle and moist, bright and shiny. The lord of the beginning cultivates the mercury. Within the sacred chamber is the empty cavern. The mysterious white gives birth to the male of metal. It occupies a strong and honored place from the start. The three and five hold on to each other. The essence flies in to moisten and nourish.

Primary Commentary

It becomes subtle and moist, bright and shiny. The lord of the beginning cultivates the mercury. Within the sacred chamber is the empty cavern.

The black lead is transformed into white metal. The essence becomes shiny and transparent. The body of the chamber of the spirit is now completed. There is an inch of emptiness in the center. This is where the true mercury is born. The lord of the beginning supervises the refining of the Golden Elixir. The *Pao-p'u-tzu* says, "The lord of the beginning speaks, 'I cultivate the elixir and become immortal.' Fu Hsi drew the pa-k'ua and Confucius described the pattern of changes. They all understood the numerics of the sky and the earth." The *Tsan-tung-chi* says, "Confucius praised the hidden changes. Ch'ien and k'un frolic in the cavern of the void."

The mysterious white gives birth to the male of metal. It occupies a strong and honored place from the start.

The subtle mystery is the creator of the white metal. Therefore it can gather and nurture the essences of the sun and the moon. Before the yang fire is kindled, it is hidden inside the white metal. Its shape and form cannot be seen. When water and fire are applied, a golden aura will emerge within the white metal. The golden aura is the harmonious vapor of wu and chi. When the two meet and merge with each other, the elixir is born. Thus the mysterious white occupies an honored place on high. These substances have existed since the ancient days. They embrace yin and yang and are a part of all things. This is the key to the Golden Elixir. Water and fire interact to create cinnabar and mercury. The bright spirit emerges. It is the mother of all things and the origin of yin and yang. This is what the *Tsan-tung-chi* means when it says, "Essence and cauldron have existed since the ancient days."

The three and five hold on to each other. The essence flies in to moisten and nourish.

The numeric of the true water of cinnabar is three and the numeric of earth is five. When water, fire, and earth interact, the sacred essence will descend into the cauldron. This is why the ancient ones built the chamber of the spirit and the cauldron. Within these vessels, male and female are coupled and the dragon and tiger are united. In the beginning, the forms are not defined and everything is undifferentiated. However, after fire is applied, the essences of husband and wife intertwine and the feelings of the dragon and the tiger are united. In this way, the sacred medicine is completed in time at the beginning of the year. The *Tsan-tung-chi* says, "The vapors of the newlyweds interlock. In the beginning of the year the sprouts are moist."

Secondary Commentary

The lords of the beginning who cultivated the elixir and attained immortality are the ancient sages. Guided by the numerics of the movement of the sky and the earth, they followed the path of the sun and the moon and built the cauldron after the structures of ch'ien and k'un. They left an inch of emptiness in the center for the numinous mercury. When movement is generated in accordance with the principles, the celestial vapor will descend and the terrestrial vapor will respond. The supreme essences of the sky and earth will copulate and create the sacred nectar. Occupying an honored position on high, it is indeed mysterious and subtle. The ancients who have attained the Tao were afraid that future generations would misunderstand the true principles and use ordinary cinnabar, quicksilver, and other substances to make the Great Elixir. They also feared that future practitioners would not know how to transform the true lead. Therefore they used metaphors to describe the making of the elixir so that future students would understand. If you use ordinary substances to make the elixir, it will be like going into the mountains to look for fish and dragons and diving into water to catch the hare. You will waste your effort and attain nothing.

Translator's Note

The numeric of the true water of cinnabar is three because the true water here refers to mercury, which is produced from cinnabar. Mercury, which is the Green Dragon of the east, belongs to the element wood, and the numeric of wood is three in the pre-creation scheme of the five elements.

13

The Mysterious Woman Unfolds the Process

The Mysterious Woman unfolds the process. Wu and chi are enhanced by the celestial fire. The celestial fire gradually runs out, following the pattern of the mysterious.

Primary Commentary

The Mysterious Woman unfolds the process. Wu and Chi are enhanced by the celestial fire.

The Mysterious Woman is the spirit and essence of the sky and the earth. She is also the numinous vapor of yin and yang. Spirit penetrates everything, but its form cannot be identified. It knows the nature of all things and understands the changes they go through. It is the guardian of the Taoist spiritual tradition. Wu and chi are vapors of harmony and are the foundations of the Great Elixir. When the celestial fire moves, the essences of wu and chi are born. The *Tsan-tung-chi* says, "The ancient sages did not live in vain. They observed the movement of the celestial bodies."

The celestial fire gradually runs out, following the pattern of the mysterious.

Celestial fire is initiated at tzu. The yang fire increases gradually. After it reaches its zenith, the celestial fire wanes at wu. The yin fire arrives gradually. Reaching hai, yin is at its zenith. At this time, the five elements are completely dissolved, the four seasons have reached the end of their cycle, and the fire has run out. This is what the *Tsan-tung-chi* means when it says, "Celestial fire has its flow and ebb. It shrinks and expands according to the hour, day, and season. The celestial mind is governed by changes."

Secondary Commentary

The Mysterious Woman is a deity from the ancient times. She is the eldest of all the immortals. Wu and chi add up to the number ten. Celestial movement is fire, and fire is the primordial vapor. When it expands, it envelops both sky and earth. When it shrinks, it is contained within a piece of hair. All living things are nourished by the primordial vapor. Expanding, the vapor encloses all things. Penetrating everything, it creates and nurtures. It controls metal and water and circulates yin and yang. It beautifies all things, and its transformations know no boundaries. Its functions are great and subtle. The enlightened ones used its sacred powers to cultivate the supreme medicine. They gathered the essences of the sun and moon and regulated the water and fire. They harmonized the warm, cool, cold, and hot. Guided by spring, summer, autumn, and winter, they were in complete harmony with the four seasons. Waxing and waning, they created the golden nectar of the sacred elixir and accomplished the subtle transformations.

Part Two

14

In Revealing the Nature of the Elixir

In revealing the nature of the elixir, there is no need to mention again the importance of ch'ien and k'un. Cinnabar is the father of mercury. Wu and chi are the mothers of yellow gold. The harmonics of the bell vibrate to the numerics of two and six. The pivot of the North Pole Star is built on three and nine. The crimson youth plays with the Red Raven, and the Green Dragon emerges in the transformation.

Primary Commentary

In revealing the nature of the elixir, there is no need to mention again the importance of ch'ien and k'un.

The nature of the Great Elixir and the method of building the chamber of the spirit have been described in the previous chapters. Therefore there is no need to repeat them here.

Cinnabar is the father of mercury. Wu and chi are the mothers of yellow gold.

Cinnabar is the sun and mercury is the spirit of the sun. Wu and chi are the moon and yellow metal is the soul of the moon. Together, cinnabar, wu, and chi give birth to the spirit and soul, thus creating the supreme medicine. Therefore they are named father and mother.

The harmonics of the bell vibrate to the numerics of two and six. The pivot of the North Pole Star is built on three and nine.

Tzu, yin, ch'en, wu, shen, and hsü are the six harmonics. Ch'ou, mao, ssu, wei, yu, and hai are the six palaces. Tzu is the yellow bell and wu is animal life. They govern the twelve segments of the day. Three and nine together make twelve. The Pole Star is the foundation. In the first month, it strengthens the terrestrial branch yin; in the second month it enhances mao, and so on through all the twelve months. The *Tsan-tung-chi* says, "Waxing and waning follow the harmonics of the bell, and ascent follows the pivot of the Pole Star."

The crimson youth plays with the Red Raven, and the Green Dragon emerges in the transformation.

The crimson youth is the sun, and the Red Raven is fire. When fire is circulated, the sun will give birth to mercury (the Green Dragon) in the chamber of the spirit. An ancient poem says, "Reverse the cycle of the five elements, and the dragon will emerge in the fire."

Secondary Commentary

T'ai-chi gives birth to the two opposites. The two opposites generate the four directions. The four directions generate the pa-k'ua, and the pa-k'ua determines fortune and misfortune. Ch'ien is sky. In stillness it is curved. In movement it is straight. K'un is earth. In stillness it is closed. In movement it is open. The classics say, "Ch'ien and k'un are the structures of the sky and earth, and k'an and li are the functions. The Tao gives birth to the sky. Sky gives birth to earth, and earth gives birth to the ten thousand things. Alternating stillness and movement, ch'ien and k'un give birth to all things."

Sky is empty. It is yang; it is hardness; and it is the sun and the father. Earth is filled. It is yin; it is softness; and it is the moon and the mother. Beneath the emptiness is earth. Above the filled space is the sky. Connecting the empty and the filled are the six yin and yang components of the hexagram. The function of ch'ien lies in the numerics seven and nine, and the function of k'un lies in the numerics six and eight. The numerics of the four directions are connected with the numerics of ch'ien and k'un. Here we see the workings of ancient yin and ancient yang and lesser yin and lesser yang. When four is paired with six, we have twenty-four. This forms the yin and yang components of ancient yin. When four is paired with eight, we have thirty-two. This forms the yin and yang components of lesser yin. When four is paired with seven, we have twenty-eight. This forms the yin and yang components of lesser yang. When four is paired with nine, we have thirty-six. This forms the yin and yang components of ancient yang. These four transformations are the work of the numerics of completion in ch'ien and k'un. The transformation of six and nine is the work of the numerics of creation in the six components of the hexagrams. The nine and six of ancient yin and ancient yang follow the changes in the hexagrams of ch'ien and k'un. The numerics seven and eight of lesser yin and lesser yang do not.

There are six components in the hexagram ch'ien and three of them belong to the earth. There are six components in the hexagram k'un and three of them belong to the sky. The hexagrams ch'ien and k'un form the basis for all the transformations in the sky and the earth. Working together constantly, they spread into the six spaces. Following the rise and fall of the vapors of yin and yang, they transform the six components of the hexagram. When ch'ien moves, it is straight and not crooked. The fire of yang starts from the ground and moves up. Transforming the lowest component of k'un, it generates the hexagram fu, which corresponds to the ninth day of the month.

It becomes the basis of movement of the six yang components of the hexagrams. In this transformation, the first faint trace of yang is born. In the second transformation, the hexagram becomes lin, as the vapor of yang begins to move. In the third transformation, the hexagram becomes t'ai, and all things emerge from the earth. In the fourth transformation, the hexagram becomes ta-ch'uang, and all things mature and grow. In the fifth transformation, the hexagram becomes kuai. All things are about to reach their full potential. When the uppermost component is transformed, the hexagram becomes the pure yang of ch'ien. At this time, the sun shines brightly and spreads through the southern positions of mao and yu. Plants blossom and the sun rises to the middle of the sky. Above, the five colors shine, and below, the water in the well is as cool as ice. All these things happen when ch'ien reaches the height of its cycle. When k'un moves, it closes but does not block. Silent and solemn, its movement begins in the sky and transforms the lowest component of ch'ien to create k'ou, which corresponds to the sixth day of the month. It becomes the basis of movement of the six yin components of the hexagrams. In this transformation, the first faint trace of yin is born. In the second transformation, the hexagram becomes tun, as the vapor of yin begins to move. In the third transformation, when the hexagram becomes pi, yin and yang are no longer connected to each other. After ripening, all things begin to fall. The fourth transformation generates the hexagram kuan, when everything decays. The fifth transformation generates po. At this time, all things hibernate and disappear. When the uppermost component is transformed, the hexagram becomes the pure yin of k'un. The essence of yin covers everything and spreads to the southern positions of mao and yu. Plants turn yellow and wither, and the essence of yin sinks heavy into the earth. The five colors are hidden in the roots, and the water in the well is warm. All these things happen when k'un reaches the height of its cycle. The classics say, "When the sun enters the earth, it is a sign that it is gathering its essence. It is transformed into fu and all things begin to grow again."

The structures of ch'ien and k'un are patterned after the vapors of yin and yang. They transform themselves by rising and falling within the six spaces. From new moon to full moon, from night to day, and through each day and month, they circulate without stopping. We do not know the extent and limits of the changes. All we know is that a harmonious vapor is responsible for the transformations. The ancient people understood the movements of the sky and the earth and were familiar with the natures of yin and yang. They formulated the method of making the elixir by observing the patterns of change and the laws of ch'ien and k'un. They regulated water and fire according to the behavior of yin and yang. They gathered the vapor of supreme harmony from the sky and the earth and channeled the pure essences of the sun and moon into the chamber of the spirit to create the golden nectar. They dissolved the mundane body and were transformed into a sacred entity. When their work was done, they became realized beings. What they accomplished was truly sacred.

Translator's Notes

The twelve hexagrams describing the waxing and waning of yin and yang are depicted in figure 6 in the introduction.

The numbers seven and nine of ch'ien add to sixteen, which is the age when males reach puberty. They represent the height of yang energy. The numbers six and eight of k'un add to fourteen, which is the age when females reach puberty. They represent the height of yin energy. Sixteen and fourteen are the numerics of the height of yang and yin energy. They symbolize eternal growth.

The products of four and six, four and eight, four and seven, and four and nine refer to applying four cycles of firing to pre-creation water (six), fire (seven), wood (eight), and metal (nine). (Refer to the translator's notes in chapter 4 for a discussion of the pre-creation numerics of the five elements.) In the firing process, the numerics of ancient yin (four times six, water) and ancient yang (four times nine, metal) follow the sequence of changes in the hexagrams, but the numerics of lesser yin (four times eight, wood) and lesser yang (four times seven, fire) do not. This means that the firing process described by the waxing and waning of yin and yang in the hexagrams pertains only to the copulation and transformation of water and metal. This particular process is described again in the next chapter, where the commentary states, "When metal and water are in position, after five days of the firing process, the vapors of the dragon and the tiger will be attracted to each other and will gather in the cauldron."

15

Initially K'un Is Transformed into Chen

Initially k'un is transformed into chen. On the third day, the moon rises in keng. East and west are separated into mao and yu. The dragon and tiger will find each other. K'un is then transformed into tui. On the eighth day, the moon rises in ting. There is half a pound of metal in the upper registers. In the third transformation, k'un becomes ch'ien. On the fifteenth day, the three yang components are in place. In roundness, they shine in the eastern position of chia. The water of metal warms the sun. The red marrow flows and becomes mercury. The new bride displays her golden splendor. The moon becomes full and then begins to wane.

Primary Commentary

Initially k'un is transformed into chen. On the third day, the moon rises in keng.

Before the new moon, at night in the hour of tzu, yang fire begins to circulate. High up, the sun and moon are in conjunction. Ch'ien interacts with the lower components of the trigram k'un to become chen. When the trigram chen directs the course of things, the first component of yang emerges at the bottom.

Therefore, on the third day of the month, the moon is in the direction of keng. This is what the *Tsan-tung-chi* means when it says, "The third day emerges smoothly. Chen takes the western position of keng."

East and west are separated into mao and yu. The dragon and tiger will find each other.

East and west are doorways to the numbers two and eight. They are the directions where the sun and moon rise. When metal and water are in position, after five days of the firing process, the vapors of the dragon and tiger will be attracted to each other and will gather in the cauldron.

K'un is then transformed into tui. On the eighth day, the moon rises in ting. There is half a pound of metal in the upper registers.

Between the sixth and the eighth day the upper registers are filled. Ch'ien interacts with the two trigram components of k'un, and the trigram tui directs the course of things. The second yang component emerges in the middle of the trigram. The moon now has half its light. The strings on the registers are as flat as ropes. The moon emerges in the position of ting. This indicates that the fire of metal in the cauldron is at half strength. The *Tsan-tung-chi* says, "On the eighth day, tui receives ting and the strings on the upper registers lie as flat as ropes."

In the third transformation, k'un becomes ch'ien. On the fifteenth day, the three yang components are in place. In roundness, they shine in the eastern position of chia.

From the thirteenth to the fifteenth day, ch'ien interacts with the upper component of k'un. Ch'ien now directs the course of things. The third yang component appears on top and the sun is round and bright. The moon appears in the direction of chia. This is a sign that, having been tempered by fire, the best metal in the cauldron is now perfect. The *Tsan-tung-chi* says, "On the fifteenth day, the structure of ch'ien is complete. It reaches its height in the eastern position of chia."

The water of metal warms the sun. The red marrow flows and becomes mercury. The new bride displays her golden splendor. The moon becomes full and then begins to wane.

When the golden nectar of the sacred elixir is at this stage of development, the essence of the sun will fill the chamber of the spirit. The vapor of the fire of metal is transformed into mercury. Mercury and its mother embrace each other and are transformed into the golden body. The souls of the frog and the rabbit are united. The light shines on the bride's body in the cauldron. Jewels are formed, radiating in golden splendor. This is a sign that the golden vapor in the cauldron has been transformed into the elixir. The *Tsan-tung-chi* says, "The croaking sound of the frog and the shadow of the rabbit brighten the two vapors. The croaking frog reveals the seasons of the hexagrams, and the soul of the rabbit emits the light of life." Between the first day and the fifteenth day, the Great Yin waxes to its full brightness. On the sixteenth day, it begins to wane. This is what the *Tsan-tung-chi* means when it says, "When seven and eight reach ssu, they bend over and descend."

(No Secondary Commentary exists for this chapter.)

Translator's Note

The number two here refers to the pre-creation fire and the number eight refers to pre-creation wood. East and west are said to be doorways because the alchemical interaction described here takes place on the east-west axis of the pre-creation pa-k'ua, between the Green Dragon and the White Tiger.

16

In Sixteen Days They Diminish

In sixteen days they diminish. Initially, ch'ien wanes to become the trigram sun. Flat and bright, the moon appears in the direction of hsin. Ch'ien continues to wane, becoming ken. On the twenty-third day, in the lower registers, water is now at half a pound. The moon rises in the southern position of ping. In the third phase of waning, ch'ien becomes k'un. K'un is complete on the thirtieth day. The northeast loses its light. The moon disappears into the earth at the position i. The moon of k'un and i is dark. Earth, wood, and metal are dissolved. Following k'un, the dragon of chen is born.

Primary Commentary

In sixteen days they diminish. Initially, ch'ien wanes to become the trigram sun. Flat and bright, the moon appears in the direction of hsin.

After sixteen days, k'un interacts with the lower component of the trigram ch'ien to become the trigram sun. When the trigram sun directs the course of things, the first yin component emerges at the bottom. The fire of yang begins to diminish and the fire of yin is born. The moon is flat and bright, appearing in the direction of hsin. The same thing occurs when the yang fire first waxes on the third day of the month. The *Tsan-tung-chi* says, "On the sixteenth day control changes hands, and the flat bright moon appears in the directions of sun [pre-creation southwest] and hsin [west]."

Ch'ien continues to wane, becoming ken. On the twenty-third day, in the lower registers, water is now at half a pound. The moon rises in the southern position of ping.

From the sixteenth day onward, the yin fire continues to descend. On the twenty-third day, k'un interacts with the middle component of ch'ien to become the trigram ken. When ken directs the course of things, the second yin component emerges in the center. The moon now appears in the direction of ping. The upper line remains the same. Metal and water each fill one-half of the cauldron. The *Tsan-tung-chi* says, "Ken is straight in the position of ping in the south. It enters the lower registers on the twenty-third."

In the third phase of waning, ch'ien becomes k'un. K'un is complete on the thirtieth day. The northeast loses its light. The moon disappears into the earth at the position i.

From the twenty-sixth to the twenty-eighth day of the month, k'un interacts with the upper component of the trigram ch'ien to become the trigram k'un. When k'un directs the course of things, the third yin component occupies the position on top. The light of the moon is about to disappear. The moon now appears in the direction of i. As for the northeast losing the light of yang, this means that brightness is dying. The *Tsan-tung-chi* says, "On the thirtieth day of k'un and i, the northeast loses its light."

The moon of k'un and i is dark. Earth, wood, and metal are dissolved. Following k'un, the dragon of chen is born.

From the twenty-eighth to the thirtieth day of the month, the fire of yin has completely run out. The vapors of yin and yang are both still. Earth, metal, and wood are brought together, becoming liquid. The vapor of the sixth yang is incompatible with the moon. The Great Yin is completely black. It travels to the northeast and then rises over the horizon. As the sun and the moon come together, water and fire are initiated again. The process returns to the beginning. The hexagram fu is once more in the lead. Following k'un, the trigram chen is born. Chen is associated with the element wood and is situated in the east. Therefore it is called the dragon. The *Tsan-tung-chi* says, "When the course of the seasons runs out, the structure renews itself, to be born again as the dragon."

Secondary Commentary

Between tzu and ssu, there are six phases in the ascent of the yang fire. They are governed by chen, tui, and ch'ien. The course of the Great Yang symbolizes the development of the golden nectar. Fu, lin, t'ai, ta-ch'uang, kuai, and ch'ien represent the course of the Great Yang and symbolize the fire of yang. Between wu and hai, there are six phases in the descent of the yin fire. They are governed by sun, ken, and k'un. The course of the Great Yin also symbolizes the development of the golden nectar. K'ou, tun, pi, kuan, po, and k'un represent the course of the Great Yin and symbolize the fire of yin. The transformation of metal and water in the cauldron is governed by the twelve hexagrams and the twelve segments of the day. The changes in the brightness of the moon correspond to the six hexagrams that govern the twelve segments of the day. The *Tsan-tung-chi* says, "It has been described in detail, but people still do not understand."

Those who want to cultivate immortality and attain the Great Elixir must understand the celestial phenomena above, the terrestrial phenomena below, and the events of humanity between. Only then can they penetrate the mystery of creation, hold yin and yang in their hands, and circulate the sun and moon in the furnace to give life to the dragon and the tiger. Ch'ien and k'un must interact in the chamber to nourish the essence of the saliva. In this way, the golden mother will not conceive the fetus in vain and the father of wood will see the day of success. The golden nectar will materialize when the body of mercury emerges. When the nine circulations are complete, the light of yang will shine with a yellow hue. It is called the bright window. It is the stone that has been transformed into gold. Ingest it and you will age with the sky. Its transformations are subtle beyond description.

17

Ch'ien and K'un Are at the Beginning and the End

Ch'ien and k'un are at the beginning and the end. Therefore they are called the dragon of chen. During the thirty days of the month, k'un gives birth to chen, tui, and ch'ien; and ch'ien gives birth to sun, ken, and k'un. The eight trigrams are arranged in their order of brightness. They move around but do not lose their center.

Primary Commentary

Ch'ien and k'un are at the beginning and the end. Therefore they are called the dragon of chen.

Ch'ien and k'un are the father and mother of all the trigrams. The two interact to create the eight. Ch'ien interacts with the lower components of the trigram k'un to become chen. This is the time of the new moon. From the hour of tzu, at midnight on the first day of the month, the fire of yang is ignited. K'un interacts with the lower components of ch'ien to become the trigram sun. From the hour of tzu, at midnight on the sixteenth day of the month, the fire of yin is ignited. Ch'ien is positioned in chia and jen and k'un is in i and kuei. The *Tsan-tung-chi* says, "Jen and kuei are matched with chia and i. Ch'ien and k'un therefore embrace both the beginning and the end."

During the thirty days of the month, k'un gives birth to chen, tui, and ch'ien; and ch'ien gives birth to sun, ken, and k'un.

K'un gives birth to the trigram chen, which directs the course of things in the first five days of the month. Next it gives birth to the trigram tui, which directs the course of things in the second five days of the month. Then it gives birth to the trigram ch'ien, which directs the course of things in the third five days of the month. The Great Yang stands erect on the fifteenth day of the month. It is full and round on top in the position of chia. The Golden Elixir in the cauldron is fully mature, its development corresponding to the sequence of changes in the trigrams. Ch'ien gives birth to the trigram sun, which directs the course of things in the first five days of the second half of the month. Next it gives birth to the trigram ken, which directs the course of things in the next five days. Then it gives birth to the trigram k'un, which directs the course of things in the last five days. The Great Yin stands high on the fifteenth day of the second half of the month. The Golden Elixir in the cauldron is solid and mature, its development corresponding to the sequence of changes in the trigrams. Throughout the thirty days of each month, ch'ien and k'un wax and wane and create and dissolve each other. The *Tsan-tung-chi* says, "The numbers seven and eight add to fifteen. So do the numbers six and nine. The four numbers together come to thirty. At this time, the vapor of yang is fully spent."

The eight trigrams are arranged in their order of brightness. They move around but do not lose their center.

As described above, the eight trigrams are arranged sequentially and matched to the thirty days of the month. They circulate the yang and yin fires and gather them into the chamber of the spirit so that the golden nectar can be transformed into the Great Elixir. The *Tsan-tung-chi* says, "The eight trigrams are displayed in their order of brightness. They move, but they do not lose their center."

Secondary Commentary

Our bodies are structured after the sky and the earth. The ascent and descent of yin and yang are patterned after the process of creation. However, when the six cravings and seven emotions are directed outward, essence and energy in the body are injured. As a result, we live in confusion all our days and do not awaken. On the contrary, if we understand the principles, live in harmony with the movement of yin and yang, and hold on to freedom and simplicity, sky and earth will copulate in the macrocosm of the universe and the microcosm of the body. The course of ascent and descent will be matched externally and internally. If we minimize thinking and do not harbor unethical thoughts, we will naturally live a long life. However, in addition to this, if we know how to set up the furnace and position the cauldron, if we follow the movement of the sky and earth, collect the essences of the sun and moon, gather the harmonious vapors of yin and yang to make the sacred medicine, and ingest it, how can we not attain immortality?

In order to create the Golden Elixir, we need to understand the nature of ch'ien and k'un and the eight trigrams. Within the thirty-day cycle of the month, the sun traverses one degree and the moon thirty degrees. When they complete their courses at the end of each month, the two end up in the same celestial palace. This is called the conjunction at the new moon. As the sun travels thirty degrees, the moon travels 395 degrees. In twelve months, the moon is with the sun in the same celestial palace. This occurs at the winter solstice. The ancient people used the numerics of the cycles of the sun and moon to schedule the firing process in each month. The first fifteen days are directed by chen, tui, and ch'ien. The last fifteen days are governed by sun, ken, and k'un. K'an and li anchor the positions, and the waxing and waning of the yang and yin fires follow accordingly. Everything is patterned after the sequence of changes in the trigrams.

TRANSLATOR'S NOTES

In the context of this chapter, the Great Yang refers to the full moon and the Great Yin refers to the dark moon. The full moon is called the Great Yang because it receives its light from the sun. Elsewhere in the book, the Great Yang is the sun and the Great Yin is the moon.

Note that the two conjunctions of the sun and moon mentioned here refer to the starting points of the lunar cycle (at new moon) and the solar cycle (at winter solstice). These are the times when the moon (yin energy) and the sun (yang energy) are renewed.

18

Regulate the Fire for Sixty Days

Regulate the fire for sixty days. The transformations will be your witness. Something like an egg will appear in the chamber of the spirit. The five mountains are connected by subterranean caverns. The pivot will be present at the great gathering.

Primary Commentary

Regulate the fire for sixty days. The transformations will be your witness.

It is difficult to recognize the primordial essence inside the cauldron. If we open the cauldron after one month, we may not find a golden aura in it. If the yin and yang fires are inadequate, the golden nectar will not materialize. Under these circumstances, another month of firing is needed to complete the elixir. The primordial essence in the cauldron is transformed when it receives external fire. Its features are difficult to discern. The twelve phases of firing correspond to changes in the hexagrams during the twelve segments of the day. They show us the sequence of movement and stillness and the patterns of flow and ebb. Therefore, the *Tsan-tung-chi* says, "It is difficult to identify the primordial essence. We need to deduce it by observing the sequence of firing."

Something like an egg will appear in the chamber of the spirit.

The wise ones of old observed the sky and the earth. The chamber of the spirit is patterned after the structures of ch'ien and k'un and is shaped like an egg. The numinous mercury is held in the one inch of emptiness. The *Tsan-tung-chi* says, "In emptiness we can see its design and give it a description."

The five mountains are connected by subterranean caverns. The pivot will be present at the great gathering.

There are five sacred mountains, and they are connected by subterranean passages. The ancient people used the shape of the mountains to guide them in building the altar, furnace, cauldron, and stove. Everything is made according to the subtle laws. All the passages are connected so that the vapor of fire can circulate smoothly. If the heat of the fire leaks out, there will be misfortune within. This is what the *Tsan-tung-chi* means when it says, "Use the shapes to guide you. Fortune and misfortune depend on knowing the firing process."

Secondary Commentary

Before sky and earth were separated, they were locked together like an egg. When they divided, the fire of yang rose and its clear and light vapor became the sky. The water of yin sank and its muddy and heavy vapor became the earth. This is known as "sky and earth occupying their positions." In the chamber of the spirit, the upper crucible is the sky and the lower crucible is the earth. When the two crucibles are joined, they are shaped like an egg. The chamber of the spirit is located in the one inch of emptiness in the center. When the sky and the earth copulate, fire is born within the water and water is born within the fire. Fire rises and water sinks. When these two substances intertwine in the true earth, the medicine is born. When there is activity in the chamber of the spirit, fire will emerge in k'an as the water leaves and sinks. When wu and chi copulate, the numinous mercury is created. These things are subtle and mysterious and you should understand them well.

19

The First Fires Are Small and Warm

The first fires are small and warm, like the initial movement of the components of the hexagrams. The top is crowned with the essence of the golden metal. The bottom carries the primordial shape of k'un. The unadorned nectar flows harmoniously in the middle. Everything is patterned after the Three Domains. The movement of ch'ien is in conjunction with the three lights. The stillness of k'un holds the vapor of yang.

Primary Commentary

The first fires are small and warm, like the initial movement of the components of the hexagrams.

The firing process of the sacred elixir follows the pattern of the components of the hexagrams as they wax and wane in the twelve months. For example, the earth-thunder hexagram of fu governs the winter solstice. The bottom component of the hexagram becomes yang at the hour of tzu. At this time, the fire is not strong. Its embers glow warmly and it is called the soft fire. This is because it is patterned after the first yang component positioned at the bottom of the fu hexagram. The *Tsan-tung-chi* says, "When initiating the first commands, do not miss the movement of the hexagram's components."

The top is crowned with the essence of the golden metal. The bottom carries the primordial shape of k'un.

The golden metal is the celestial realm of ch'ien. It is the upper crucible. The primordial k'un is earth. It is the lower crucible. When the two crucibles are locked together, they become the chamber of the spirit. The *Tsan-tung-chi* says, "Observe the river pattern above and scrutinize the flow of the earth below."

The unadorned nectar flows harmoniously in the middle. Everything is patterned after the Three Domains.

When the chamber of the spirit is in place, the unadorned nectar of the numinous mercury will be born within. The numinous middle palace is the place where the spirit of the heart resides. When sky, earth, and humanity are all present, the ten thousand things can be named. All this is possible because of the properties of metal and wood. The *Tsan-tung-chi* says, "The harmonious middle is in the heart of humanity. Everything is patterned after the Three Domains."

The movement of ch'ien is in conjunction with the three lights. The stillness of k'un holds the vapor of yang.

Ch'ien is the sky, the sun, and fire. When the primordial ch'ien moves, the essences of fire and wood will be created within the void to become the golden nectar. K'un is earth, moon, and water. Primordial k'un resides in stillness. The essences of water, metal, and moon are harmonized with the pearls of the sun. Everything is enclosed so that nothing can leak out. The *Tsan-tung-chi* says, "Movement is initiated in accordance with the cycle of the hexagrams. Stillness is patterned after the order of the hexagrams. Ch'ien and k'un govern the applications. The behavior of sky and earth follows accordingly. How can you not take note of this?"

Secondary Commentary

The sun is li. Its position is in the south and it resides in ping and ting. These are the true locations of fire. Fire is enclosed in the sun. Subsequently, it is transformed into mercury. Therefore it is said that mercury emerges from the sun. Mercury is the spirit of yang. The components of the trigram li are two yang and one yin. The earth of chi is its spirit. It is the middle daughter of k'un. The light of the sun comes from the earth of chi. Chi is associated with yin. Therefore its pattern matches the trigram li. Hidden in the light of the sun is the subtle hue of red. Its transformation from green into red is symbolized by the red cinnabar. The moon is associated with k'an. Its position is in the north and it resides in jen and kuei. These are the true locations of water. Water is embodied in the moon. When transformed, it becomes the body of metal. Therefore it is said that metal is created from the moon. Metal is the soul of yin. The components of the trigram k'an are two yin and one yang. The earth of wu is its spirit. It is the middle son of ch'ien. The moon draws its essence from the wu of earth. The wu of earth is associated with yang. Therefore its pattern matches the trigram k'an. Hidden in the essence of moon is the unadorned color of black. The transformation of white into black is symbolized by the black lead. Mercury has within it the vapor of li. It is patterned after the positions of the yin components of that trigram. Mercury is not ordinary quicksilver or cinnabar. It is something that emerges from the Great Yang of li and it is called the spirit of water. This is the true mercury. Lead has within it the vapor of k'an. It is patterned after the yang components of that trigram. Lead is not ordinary metal found in the salt beds and rocks. It is something that emerges from the Great Yin or k'an. It is called white metal and it is the true lead. When lead divides, the two opposites make up the chamber of the spirit. Mercury is born from the numeric one. It is the vapor of the mysterious nectar. All these substances are patterned after the Three Domains, which are sky, earth, and humanity.

Part Three

20

Begin the Work in the Chamber of the Spirit

Begin the work in the chamber of the spirit. The Golden Elixir will gradually materialize. Everything must be stable. The refined vapor flies around in the enclosure. The numinous doorway opens and closes. In the realm of the inaudible and invisible, creation occurs in the cavity of the deep spring.

Primary Commentary

Begin the work in the chamber of the spirit. The Golden Elixir will gradually materialize.

Once the chamber of the spirit is built and the methods are understood, there will be no problem in completing the Golden Elixir.

Everything must be stable. The refined vapor flies around in the enclosure.

Those who cultivate the elixir must first know how to seal the cauldron and not let the numinous mercury dissipate. Then the elixir can be completed.

The numinous doorway opens and closes. In the realm of the inaudible and invisible, creation occurs in the cavity of the deep spring.

The chamber of the spirit consists of an upper and a lower crucible. When it is open, it is divided into two parts. When closed, it becomes one. In the empty space within, water and fire interact and the sacred substance is born. It is inaudible and invisible. The white metal creates quicksilver and becomes an elixir. It is called the golden nectar. The place where the elixir resides is called the cavity of the nadir.

Secondary Commentary

The water of the north creates white metal, which is the true lead. It is the supreme essence of yin that contains the harmonious yang. Flowing with the primordial vapor that creates all things, it always returns to its origin. People in the ancient times were guided by the patterns of creation in the sky and the earth. They returned the harmonious vapor of yang to the true lead. Following the laws of nature, they created the Great Medicine. This is the true primordial vapor, which cannot be manufactured from mundane substances. If you follow the methods and understand the principles of cultivation, how can you not succeed in making the Great Elixir?

The dragon and tiger are both created in the lead. The rise and fall of water and fire cause metal and wood to interact in the domain of the inaudible and invisible. The sun and moon meet in the cavity of creation, where the white metal is the mother. Embracing the spirit of all things, it gives birth to the supreme treasure.

21

The Vapor of Yang Activates K'un

The vapor of yang activates k'un. The image of the sun is at the extreme south. The five stars (planets) are strung together like pearls. The sun and moon are in conjunction. The grains of the golden cinnabar are separated. Inhalation and exhalation are in harmony.

Primary Commentary

The vapor of yang activates k'un. The image of the sun is at the extreme south.

At the end of the month of hai, the pure yin of k'un has completed its course. In the beginning of the month of tzu, at midnight in the hour of tzu, a yang component emerges at the bottom of the hexagram of k'un, and the hexagram fu is born. This is when the yang fire is initiated. Continuing from ch'ou through the hours of yin to ssu, the vapor of yang reaches its height in the south. Then yin is born in the hour of wu.

The five stars (planets) are strung together like pearls. The sun and moon are in conjunction.

The five stars (planets) move through the sky like a string of pearls. Sometimes their movement is fast; sometimes it is slow. Sometimes they stop moving; sometimes they hide. At other times, they move clockwise, counterclockwise, forward, and backward. The paths of the sun and moon intersect once a month. Their conjunctions with the five stars are documented in the charts. At this time, in the beginning of the year, they are ready for metal and fire to use.

The grains of the golden cinnabar are separated. Inhalation and exhalation are in harmony.

The golden cinnabar is the essence of the sun and moon. The rise and fall of water and fire constitute one cycle of movement and stillness. The golden cinnabar floats and sinks in the cauldron in accordance with the application of external fire and in synchrony with inhalation and exhalation.

Secondary Commentary

The true lead is the mother. It is k'un. The body of the Great Yin is always dark. Its form emerges only when it encounters the fire of yang. Once its form materializes, it travels the course of the sixty-four hexagrams through the 384 yin and yang components. Its myriad transformations follow the numerics of the sun, the moon, and the five stars (planets). If you use miscellaneous mundane substances to make the elixir, how can you be renewed by the yin and yang of the four seasons?

22

The Glorious Dome Covers the Top

The glorious dome covers the top. The Three Altars support from below. The ones who direct destiny and grant prosperity are securely hidden. They determine whether debts need to be paid.

Primary Commentary

The glorious dome covers the top. The Three Altars support from below. The ones who direct destiny and grant prosperity are securely hidden. They determine whether debts need to be paid.

The sixteen stars of the glorious dome are shaped like a lid. The stars in the palace of the star Tzu-wei make up the throne of the ruler. The six stars of the Three Altars constellation are outside the palace of Tzu-wei. They regulate yin and yang and direct the transformations of all things. Water and fire reside in the upper and lowers parts of the golden cauldron. If the transformations go according to the principles, the sacred essence will be born within. The stars of the Three Altars constellation govern destiny and grant prosperity. Wen-ch'ang is the commander of the armies and the chief minister. When the waxing and the waning of the five stars (planets) are irregular, the movement of the sun and moon will be erratic. The four seasons will not behave properly. Wind and rain will be untimely, and the myriad things will not grow. Similarly, if those who cultivate the elixir deviate from the schedule of the firing process, the cauldron will be either too masculine or too feminine. As a result, the transformations will be erratic, and the project of cultivating the elixir will fail. Familiarize yourself with the instructions until you can recite them easily. Seal the cauldron and make sure that there are no leaks. Deviation from one principle will cause you to accumulate debts. The *Tsan-tung-chi* says, "Wen-ch'ang judges the amount of prosperity and the Altars and Guardians determine the amount of debts. The hundred officials all have duties, each performing the functions of their departments."

Secondary Commentary

Many people try to learn the arts of the Tao, but only one or two out of a thousand penetrate the subtleties. Some use their skills to take advantage of others and benefit themselves. Some attempt to transform the yellow and white through heat and combustion. Some try to entice keng and ken to achieve a union. Some claim authority from the ancient classics. They refine the five metals and the eight minerals, hoping to create the Great Medicine. In the end, they waste their time and energy and accomplish nothing. The foolish ones accumulate more folly and the intelligent ones waste their talents. They cling to their actions until death and never wake up from ignorance. In confusion they pass their methods to future generations. This continues endlessly. As a result, many people lose their jobs, their property, and their savings. They neglect their filial duties and forget the welfare of their spouse and children. They wander around, searching aimlessly. You see these kinds of people in every generation. They do not know that the Great Medicine of the Golden Elixir cannot be manufactured with ordinary lead and mercury. They do not know that the essences of the sky and the earth, and the spirit and soul of the sun and the moon, are the necessary ingredients. The problem with them is that they do not build the foundations with that which is in their territory.

Translator's Note

The sixteen stars that make up the lid are the seven stars of the Northern Bushel (the Big Dipper), the North Pole Star, the Left and Right Guardian stars, and the six stars of the Three Altars.

23

Earth in the Central Palace Is Tempered by Fire

Earth in the Central Palace is tempered by fire. Metal enters the water of the north. The three elements water, earth, and metal undergo transformation for sixty days. Everything must occur naturally. They should first be preserved and then extinguished. If the fire is too strong, the effects will be halved. If the quicksilver is unstable, it may stay together or separate. If hardness and softness conflict and do not penetrate each other, it is not the fault of fire. Rather, earth is to blame.

Primary Commentary

Earth in the Central Palace is tempered by fire. Metal enters the water of the north.

Fire is sun and metal is moon. It is natural that the birth of metal and fire follows the movement of the vapors of the five elements and the six harmonics. Thus fire gives birth to earth, and metal gives birth to water. Each emits its essence to make the sacred medicine. The *Tsan-tung-chi* says, "The sun is in harmony with the essence of the five elements and the moon is guided by the six harmonics."

The three elements water, earth, and metal undergo transformation for sixty days.

There is only one substance, the mother of metal, in the Central Palace. Water and earth are united when they are subjected to the firing process. If fire is applied for one month and the golden nectar is not in synchrony with the root numerics, it will be necessary to start the fires again the next month. The *Tsan-tung-chi* says, "Five and six yield thirty phases. Let the phases return to the beginning again."

Everything must occur naturally. They should first be preserved and then extinguished.

The secret of the golden nectar and the sacred elixir lies in the firing process. Fire is the father and mother of the medicine. The medicine is the grandchild of fire, for it is born naturally from the vapors of the sky and earth. It is possible that the golden mercury will be born when the fire stops. But if fire is applied inaccurately, everything will be lost. The golden nectar is unstable. Therefore it is necessary to watch its beginning and end during the sixty days. The *Tsan-tung-chi* says, "Return to the beginning and determine the end. This is the key to its existence."

If the fire is too strong, the effects will be halved.

If yang fire is too strong, the spirit's vapor will be damaged. The golden mercury will overflow after it has filled the cauldron. This happens when we deviate from the correct formula. The *Tsan-tung-chi* says, "When the ruler is negligent, things will leave their path and become excessive."

If the quicksilver is unstable, it may stay together or separate.

Quicksilver is the Golden Elixir. If it is insufficiently heated, the quicksilver in the cauldron will fluctuate with the heat of the fire. Subsequently, its movement will deviate from the correct pathway. Sometimes it will separate and sometimes it will stay together. As a result, we will not be able to predict when the elixir will emerge. The *Tsan-tung-chi* says, "If the subordinates are devious and unruly, the movement will not follow the correct path."

If hardness and softness conflict and do not penetrate each other, it is not the fault of fire. Rather, earth is to blame.

If the golden cinnabar does not measure to the correct numerics, and hardness and softness do not penetrate each other, it is not the fault of fire. Rather, it is because there are impurities in the mother of metal in the Central Palace. The fault lies in the inadequacy of essence and vapor. Therefore it is not fire that should be blamed but earth. The *Tsan-tung-chi* says, "When you see that some things are sufficient and others are inadequate, you are disappointed that the transformation has gone wrong. You pinpoint the culprit and put the blame on the responsible party."

Secondary Commentary

Those who cultivate the elixir must understand the numerics of the phases of the sun and moon, the principles of the flow and ebb of yin and yang, and the application of fire and heat. They must also recognize the difference between the true and the false ingredients. Then they will succeed in their endeavor. The key to success lies in the firing process. Those who circulate the fire but do not understand its secret will not be able to get a good grasp of the method. What they will teach will be false. Their actions will be a mockery of the teachings of the elders and they will never awaken from ignorance. Those who wish to attain the Tao should beware of such pitfalls.

24

Earth Guards the Central Palace

Earth guards the Central Palace and envelops the four directions. The three lights are in harmony with each other and peace is established. The five viscera are nourished within. The four limbs are balanced. Water freezes and fire is extinguished. The glow is hidden but there is a radiance within. Metal and wood support each other. The elusive brightness is concealed inside. Set the water at the right temperature and stoke the fire. Initiate the process and everything will be transformed. The Tao is now close and within reach.

Primary Commentary

Earth guards the Central Palace and envelops the four directions.

Earth is wu and chi, and mother. The mother resides in the Central Palace. She collects the harmonious vapors from the four directions and puts them into the chamber of the spirit to be transformed into the golden nectar. The *Tsan-tung-chi* says, "When ssu has reached its height, the commands are issued. The mother of metal can leisurely gather the officers and citizens. Therefore it is said that when ssu reaches its height, the commands are issued and orders are leisurely given to the subordinates."

The three lights are in harmony with each other and peace is established.

The three lights are the sun, moon, and stars. If their movements in the sky follow the correct paths, there will be peace in the celestial realm and on earth. Yang fire, yin water, and the fetus of metal are patterned after the sun, moon, and stars. The movements of the three lights correspond to movement and stillness in the components of the hexagrams. If the yin and yang fires are circulated correctly, there will be no harm. It will be like a country in times of peace. The *Tsan-tung chi* says, "When everything is bright, virtue will stand upright, and no harm will come to the nation."

The five viscera are nourished within. The four limbs are balanced.

If the circulation of fire follows the numerics of celestial movement, the realized being will emerge in the cauldron. The five viscera will be regulated and the four limbs will be relaxed. Emptiness and simplicity will reign in the center, and there will be no threat of danger and loss. The *Tsan-tung-chi* says, "Nourish yourself within and maintain stillness and emptiness."

Water freezes and fire is extinguished. The glow is hidden but there is a radiance within.

In the process of cultivating the Great Elixir, water freezes in the hour of ssu and fire is extinguished in the hour of hai. During these times, the essence and vapor of metal and fire are drawn toward each other. A glowing light is diffused throughout the chamber, illuminating the body of the enlightened being. The *Tsan-tung-chi* says, "The origin glows with a faint light and illuminates the true body within."

Metal and wood support each other. The elusive brightness is concealed inside.

The vapors of the dragon and tiger interact. The feelings of metal and wood unite. When metal subdues wood and wood is controlled by metal, wood will flourish. Its splendor is locked inside the cauldron, for the root of the spirit is concealed in the chamber. All this is made possible by the nourishing nature of the mother of metal. However, the behavior of the mother of metal is unpredictable. Subtle and mysterious, the instructions cannot be transmitted verbally. The *Tsan-tung-chi* says, "Conceal its glow and strengthen the root of the spirit."

Set the water at the right temperature and stoke the fire. Initiate the process and everything will be transformed. The Tao is now close and within reach.

Inside the cauldron, the mother of metal swallows the vapors of the three lights, gathers the essences of the sun and moon, and conceives the sacred fetus. The form of the fetus is intangible. The seed of the pearl and the numinous mercury are enclosed in the chamber of the spirit. Their existence can barely be discerned. If the applications of water and fire are timely, water and fire will descend and ascend in the correct way. If everything works according to the celestial order and the natural principles, metal and mercury will be attracted to each other, and the dragon and tiger will copulate. The principles are revealed in the changing phenomena and the rules of transformations. The *Tsan-tung-chi* says, "The three lights submerge to incubate the seed of the pearl. It cannot be seen, yet it is close and easy to attain."

Secondary Commentary

We can deduce the principles of creation. If the essence of the three lights has not emerged, if the vapors of the four seasons are not separated, if the mysterious yellow is undifferentiated, and if the clear and the muddy are together, the vapor of the true lead must still be embraced by the undifferentiated whole. When what is clear has become sky and what is muddy has become earth, the harmony of yin and yang will produce humanity. When the positions of the Three Domains are established, the vapor of the true lead will move to the center to occupy the position of wu and chi. This is the mother of the sacred medicine. It envelops the four directions. The vapors of metal, wood, water, and fire come together to form the golden nectar. In the cycle of the five elements, metal subdues wood. Inside wood is fire. Fire subdues metal. Metal and water mutually control each other and become strong. Water subdues fire, but inside, fire is the earth that controls water. When water and earth interact, they are both transformed. These are the principles of creation and dissolution. These instructions can only be transmitted as mnemonics. They cannot be recorded in detail. If you understand the laws of the celestial order, you will realize that what we are talking about is the breath of the original harmonious vapor.

25

When Water Is Coupled with Earth

When water is coupled with earth, clouds of emerald haze are born. The yellow and black are mixed with the original undifferentiated essence, and a purple aura surrounds the sun. Water gives birth to the ten thousand things. These secrets are known only to the sages.

Primary Commentary

When water is coupled with earth, clouds of emerald haze are born.

Water is the mysterious water and earth is the mother of metal. When the fire of the sun copulates with the mother of metal, the essence of wood is transformed into vapor in the chamber of the spirit. Wisps of clouds appear, and the smooth round pearl will gradually crystallize and moisten the palace of the elixir. It will then be tranformed into the golden nectar. The *Tsan-tung-chi* says, "The yellow in the center gradually unfolds according to the principles, and moisture spreads to the skin and muscles."

The yellow and black are mixed with the original undifferentiated essence, and a purple aura surrounds the sun.

Yellow and black are associated respectively with earth and water. When the vapors of water and earth subdue each other, the original essence of the sun will be born. If everything works according to the subtle principles, the original essence of the sun will hover between existence and nothingness. When the foundations are complete, a purple aura will surround the sun. If the yellow nectar swirls about, it is a sign that the sacred medicine is still unstable. The *Tsan-tung-chi* says, "In the beginning, you do not know what will be the outcome, because the supports are not in place."

Water gives birth to the ten thousand things. These secrets are known only to the sages.

The numeric of water is one. The mystery in the sky gives birth to water and places it in the north. Metal is embodied in water, but it also gives birth to water. The sages knew about these things. Guided by the patterns of the natural order, they created the sacred elixir. It is something that less intelligent people cannot fathom. This is what the *Tsan-tung-chi* means when it says, "The numeric one is hidden. People do not know about it."

Secondary Commentary

The structures of ch'ien and k'un embody all the subtle phenomena. Water created by the numeric one of the sky is called the mysterious water. Earth created by the numeric five of earth is called the true earth. Water and earth interact to create the ten thousand things. The sages knew about these things. They patterned the chamber of the spirit after the structures of the sky and earth. They applied the laws of yin and yang to regulate the water and fire. They observed the four seasons and followed the changes described by the hexagrams. Eventually the original essence was born and the sacred mercury emerged.

26

The Best Metal Is Initially White

The best metal is initially white. Refine it, and it will turn yellow. Tame it, and it will be transformed in the Central Palace. Locked inside, the yellow metal does not fly out. Smoke and clouds rise as earth is set on fire.

PRIMARY COMMENTARY

The best metal is initially white. Refine it, and it will turn yellow.

Lead is refined to become white metal. White metal is the chamber of the spirit. Inside the chamber is the water of metal. When the water of metal is transformed by fire, its color changes to yellow, and it is called the yellow cart. The *Tsan-tung-chi* says, "Below is the vapor of the sun. Cover and incubate it within. First it liquifies; then it coagulates. It is called the yellow cart."

Tame it, and it will be transformed in the Central Palace. Locked inside, the yellow metal does not fly out. Smoke and clouds rise as earth is set on fire.

When the golden nectar emerges, it follows the path of water and fire and is gathered into the container. Gold is transformed into a liquid and it is then crystallized in the Central Palace. Thus the golden nectar cannot escape. The fire burns with a golden glow. Its vapor is clear and it floats around like a thin layer of mist. Its transformations in the chamber of the cauldron are unpredictable. It can appear as an infant sucking a breast or as the fangs of an animal. It can appear as the sun and moon, revealing their spirit and soul. It can take on the forms of the dragon and tiger. This is what happens when metal and wood interact. The spirit assumes countless forms that are indescribable. If you had used common substances such as five metals and eight minerals, how could you have produced these kinds of magical transformations?

Secondary Commentary

Of all the substances, only yellow metal is indestructible. From the beginning of time, the body of gold cannot be harmed. Therefore the mother of the golden metal is called the true lead. True lead was born before the sky was created. When everything was still undifferentiated, the vapor of lead was already present. When sky and earth separated, the structure of lead emerged. If the ten thousand myriad things do not have in them the vapor of lead, they cannot perform their functions. Thus the vapor of true lead is in everything. Black metal gives birth to white metal; white metal gives birth to yellow metal; and yellow metal gives birth to the supreme medicine. Ingest it, and you will age with the sky and earth and embody the structure of the Tao. Therefore the essence of the best metal is the ruler of all the herbs and the ancestor of all things.

27

Substance and Nonsubstance Subdue Each Other

Substance and nonsubstance subdue each other. Above is the residence of the Green Dragon. The two nonsubstances originate from substance. The numinous transformations are difficult to enumerate.

PRIMARY COMMENTARY

Substance and nonsubstance subdue each other. Above is the residence of the Green Dragon.

White metal is substantive. The vapor of fire is nonsubstantive. Thus, substance and nonsubstance subdue each other. Metal and water interact to create the numinous mercury in the Central Palace. Mercury is the Green Dragon. The *Tsan-tung-chi* says, "The upper enclosure is substantive and the lower enclosure is nonsubstantive. Thus nonsubstance supports substance. Above is the residence of the spirit."

The two nonsubstances originate from substance. The numinous transformations are difficult to enumerate.

The two nonsubstances are the vapors of yin and yang and the spirit and soul of the sun and moon. They make up the womb of the spirit. There are no mundane substances inside the womb of the spirit. It is empty. The vapors of water and fire are used to direct the essences of the sun and moon and gather the supreme yin and yang into the womb of the spirit. The numinous transformations of the golden nectar are hard to predict. The water and fire in the upper and lower halves of the chamber of the spirit emerge when the mother of metal conceives. The *Tsan-tung-chi* says, "This is the method of the two openings that requires the vapor of metal."

Secondary Commentary

The golden nectar is called the yellow cart. It also refers to the Nine Circulations. When the ancient sages ingested the elixir or medicine, they purified themselves and the surroundings before they swallowed the pill. When the inner and outer environments are in harmony with each other, the true vapor will be heated and channeled to the four extremities. Youthfulness will be recovered. The body will be filled with pure yang, and longevity will match that of the sky.

28

Refine the Silver in the Lead

Refine the silver in the lead and the sacred substance will emerge. Silver is the essence of gold, and lead embodies the spirit of the north. Water is the pivot of the Tao. Its number is one and it is the origin of yin and yang. Therefore it has within it the essence of silver. Lead is transformed into the yellow elixir. It takes its place among the five minerals. Lead is black on the outside. It takes on the color of north. Inside it is the essence of gold. It hides a piece of jade within, but externally it is a wild man.

Primary Commentary

Refine the silver in the lead and the sacred substance will emerge.

Before white metal has developed its form, it is hidden in the mysterious water of the north. If we recognize the white metal, we can extract it from the black lead and use it to build the foundations of the Great Medicine. Initiate the process according to the order of things and the sacred substance will emerge. This is what the *Tsan-tung-chi* means when it says, "Know the white and hold on to the black. The bright spirit will naturally come."

Silver is the essence of gold, and lead embodies the spirit of the north.

White metal is the essence of metal. The true lead is the foundation of the mysterious water. Within it is the true quicksilver of the north. The *Tsan-tung-chi* says, "White is the essence of metal and black is the foundation of water."

Water is the pivot of the Tao. Its number is one and it is the origin of yin and yang. Therefore it has within it the essence of silver.

White metal is born from water. Use it as the sacred container, and the body of water will not be exhausted. The attraction of metal and water forms the pivot and is the origin of yin and yang. Therefore it is called the essence of silver. The essence of silver is the medicine. The *Tsan-tung-chi* says, "Water is the pivot of the Tao. Its number is one. It is the origin of yin and yang."

Lead is transformed into the yellow elixir. It takes its place among the five minerals.

Lead is also called the mysterious one. It occupies the position of k'an. The vapors of water, fire, metal, and wood are hidden in lead. Lead is the ruler of the five metals and eight minerals. When the liquid pearl encounters it, the foundation is built. This results from compounding the vapors of water and fire. The *Tsan-tung-chi* says, "Enclosed in the lead is the yellow sprout, the ruler of the five metals. It is the waterwheel of the north."

Lead is black on the outside. It takes on the color of north. Inside it is the essence of gold.

Lead is black outside but there is a golden aura inside. It resides in the jen and kuei positions of the north. The *Tsan-tung-chi* says, "Lead is black externally but internally it has a golden aura."

It hides a piece of jade within, but externally it is a wild man.

Before the true lead is cultivated and refined, it is mixed with other minerals in the mine. Therefore it is described as black on the outside but hiding a treasure within. The *Tsan-tung-chi* says, "Hidden within is a piece of jade. Externally it is a wild man."

Secondary Commentary

The cauldron is the medicine and the medicine is the cauldron. Cauldron and medicine are one and the same thing. If the golden nectar could be made from mundane substances, many people would have attained immortality by ingesting them. Thus the *Tsan-tung-chi* says, "Do not use force. Abandon the eight minerals." This is because it knows that the Great Elixir cannot be compounded from the mundane five metals and eight minerals.

Sometimes we see traces of green in the essences of the male and female. Sometimes the color of the Golden Elixir turns from red to purple. This is because it is tinted by the greenish vapor of the male and female. The natural and original vapor gives life to grass, trees, leaves, and fruits. The hues are vivid and are not tinted by the greenish colors of the male and female. An old poem says, "Flowers bloom in the most unusual ways. In the midst of green leaves are bright red buds. No one can tint these colors. They are produced by the fires of transformation." The blossoming of the flowers and leaves is part of the natural order of things and is the work of the vapors of water, fire, and earth. It is the same with the Golden Elixir. It follows the laws of creation in the sky and earth and is in harmony with the natural ways of metal and wood. If you can bring together water, fire, and earth, how can you not generate the transformations? Many people look for formulas to compound ordinary metals and minerals. They do not know how to use the real ingredients of the golden mercury and numinous nectar. Only those who truly cultivate the Great Elixir will understand the mysteries of the Tao and know where the true lead is produced.

They are the ones who will succeed in making the golden nectar. Therefore the immortal Liu Chih-ku says, "The dragon and tiger are metal and mercury. If you follow the natural principles to gather the golden nectar and ingest it, how can you not become immortal?"

29

Silver Is the Mother of Lead

Silver is the mother of lead; the mother hides in the lead. Lead is the child of silver; the child is enclosed in the womb of the silver. The true simplicity is subtle and elusive. Sometimes it exists and sometimes it does not. In the hot fires of the charcoal pit, lead sinks and silver rises. Pure and white, it appears like a jewel, and can be used to construct the yellow cart.

Primary Commentary

Silver is the mother of lead; the mother hides in the lead.

Silver is metal and lead is water. Water is born inside metal but metal is also the mother of water. However, metal is hidden inside the water of lead. The *Tsan-tung-chi* says, "Metal is the mother of water, and the mother hides in the womb of its child."

Lead is the child of silver; the child is enclosed in the womb of the silver.

Silver is the child. It is also water. Lead is the mother. It is also metal. Metal gives birth to water, and its child (water) returns to reside in the mother (lead). This is why it is called the black lead. The *Tsan-tung-chi* says, "Water is the child of metal, and the child is enclosed in the mother's womb." After lead is transformed, it resides in the west and hides inside water. Nourished by water, it matures and is called the black lead. When it is refined into white metal, it becomes the chamber of the spirit. When yang fire is applied, water will flow out from the white metal and the true quicksilver will emerge. This true substance is the one breath that created the sky and the earth.

The true simplicity is subtle and elusive. Sometimes it exists and sometimes it does not.

The true simplicity is the true mercury in the mother's womb. Receiving the heat of the external fire, it sometimes appears and sometimes disappears. Floating and sinking unpredictably, it is hidden in the chamber of the cauldron. Therefore its form cannot be seen. The *Tsan-tung-chi* says, "The realized being is extremely subtle. Sometimes it exists and sometimes it does not."

In the hot fires of the charcoal pit, lead sinks and silver rises.

When fire is ignited in the charcoal pit, lead sinks and silver rises. This is the white metal. The immortal Chen-i says that this is the true mercury of the sacred cauldron. When it is heated by the fires of rising yang and falling yin, it flies about unpredictably. Sometimes it floats and sometimes it sinks. The chamber of the spirit is like a large lake. The *Tsan-tung-chi* says, "Floating around in the great lake, it sometimes sinks and sometimes rises."

Pure and white, it appears like a jewel, and can be used to construct the yellow cart.

White metal is tempered in the charcoal pit. The white metal can be used to build the chamber of the spirit and the yellow cart. The *Tsan-tung-chi* says, "Gather it and it is white. Build with it and it is red."

Secondary Commentary

The key to the golden nectar lies in the sacred water of the celestial pool (hua-chi). The celestial pool is the mother of metal. Metal is the white metal of the west. Inside the metal is a liquid. This is mercury. Although the sun and the liquid pearl have different functions, they come from the same origin. The supreme beings used metal to cultivate mercury and transform it into cinnabar powder. This is the natural way of returning to the origin of things. White metal and the spirit mother are cultivated and transformed into the Great Elixir. When the Great Elixir is complete, saliva and moisture will flow without stopping. Therefore it is called the golden nectar. Those who wish to attain the Tao should heed this: do not compound quicksilver and metals found in the mountains and lakes and think that this is cultivating mercury.

30

Grain Is the Essence of Metal

Grain is the essence of metal. Water becomes the yellow fluid. It travels to the area measuring one inch square and merges with the Three Domains. Like sky and earth before separation, it is shaped like an egg.

Primary Commentary

Grain is the essence of metal. Water becomes the yellow fluid.

The true lead is refined into white metal. The white metal is the cauldron. It is the mother of the essence of metal. Inside it is quicksilver, which can be transformed into the yellow fluid. The *Tsan-tung-chi* says, "Refine it and guard it. Within the white is the real substance."

It travels to the area measuring one inch square and merges with the Three Domains.

The chamber of the spirit is the space in the center that measures one inch square. The upper crucible is the sky and the lower crucible is the earth. In the middle is the numinous mercury. These three are patterned after the Three Domains. The

Tsan-tung-chi says, "The square measures one inch. Here, things are undifferentiated and are intertwined with each other."

Like sky and earth before separation, it is shaped like an egg.

Before the sky and earth were separated, they were undifferentiated and shaped like an egg. Inside, the essences of the sun and moon interact and the forms of the ten thousand things are created. The enlightened ones described the chamber of the spirit as an undifferentiated whole and patterned it after the structures of the Three Domains. Letting the yang fire ascend and the yin fire descend, they conserved the essences of the sun and the moon. The true lead was born before sky and earth were separated. It must be gathered with the right method and made according to the correct principles. The process cannot be rushed. The *Tsan-tung-chi* says, "It was born before the sky and the earth and it occupies an honored place on high."

Secondary Commentary

When white metal emerges, it is shaped like the tooth of a white horse. It likes to eat the essence of wood. Wood is born from the water of the north. After it is refined, it appears white as snow. It is the treasured elixir. The immortal T'ao says, "Use the treasure to refine the treasure. Those who persevere will attain the Tao." Ko Ya-ch'üan says, "The ghost hides within the nectar of stone. The essence of metal is covered by the mountain. Scrutinize it and it appears as a white jewel." When it can be described as pure and white as a jewel, it is ready to be made into the golden nectar of the sacred elixir.

People today heat ordinary cinnabar and quicksilver. Even if the firing process is followed correctly, these substances will not change their nature. If ingested, the cinnabar will not enter the five viscera. Instead, it will dissipate like mist in the wind and rain.

31

Something Rises from the Sphere

Something rises from the sphere. It is shaped like a Peng-lai jug. Locked and secured inside, the spirit circulates. The design is patterned after a furnace. It is concealed and guarded. In control and wrapped around itself, it is protected from harm. All this is a part of the natural way, for the transformations of the spirit are limitless.

PRIMARY COMMENTARY

Something rises from the sphere. It is shaped like a Peng-lai jug.

In the cultivation of the Great Elixir, the furnace and the cauldron must be positioned so that the upper and lower components are connected to form the shape of a jug. The *Tsan-tung-chi* says, "Locked all around, it is like a sealed jug."

Locked and secured inside, the spirit circulates.

Everywhere inside the cauldron is connected so that the vapor of fire can be circulated. When the substances meet inside, they are secured so that nothing can escape. The *Tsan-tung-chi* says, "It is locked in on all sides. Within the hearth, every place is connected."

The design is patterned after a furnace. It is concealed and guarded.

On the altar is the furnace. On the furnace is a container. In the container is the cauldron, and within the cauldron is the chamber of the spirit. Inside the chamber of the spirit are metal and water. They are wrapped around each other so that destructive influences cannot enter. This allows the numinous mercury to develop. The *Tsan-tung-chi* says, "Everything is guarded securely. All malevolent influences are eradicated."

In control and wrapped around itself, it is protected from harm.

The golden cauldron is contained in the hearth. Connected to the four directions, it allows the vapor of fire to circulate. Water is positioned on top of the golden cauldron. Fire is circulated below it. Altar, furnace, cauldron, and hearth are tightly intertwined so that unexpected and unwanted influences cannot enter. The *Tsan-tung-chi* says, "The twisted passages are all connected. In this way, nothing disastrous can happen."

All this is a part of the natural way, for the transformations of the spirit are limitless.

The substances that make up the Great Medicine are the essences of the sun, moon, and stars. The golden nectar is made from the vapors of the five elements and four directions. Other than these things, nothing else is involved.

Secondary Commentary

The enlightened ones pitied those who are drowning in ignorance. Many die because they do not know where the spirit is located. They do not understand the nature of the mind nor recognize the key to the golden nectar. Therefore the sages have transmitted the teachings to humanity. The Yellow Emperor and Lao-tzu both followed these methods and became the teachers of later generations. They ingested the elixir and attained longevity. They transformed themselves so that they could enter fire and not be burned and stay under water and not drown. The emperors of the ancient times also knew about these methods and taught them. Therefore, in those days, people did not have to travel to foreign countries to learn the arts of immortality. The later generations lost much of this knowledge. Their learning became shallow. As a result, the methods became secret. During the Chou dynasty, Lao-tzu came among humanity. When he was about to leave for the frontier, he transmitted the teachings to Wen-tzu, a guard at the city gates. Now these teachings are among us and are taught to those who are destined to learn them. In this way, the seed of the Tao will not be lost.

People today do not know better. They pamper their bodies with wealth; they let fame and fortune imprison their minds; they let wine and meats block their breath; and they let sexual desire confuse their feelings. They revel in the four delights and are afraid of death. Wanting to lengthen their life span, they seek the masters of the formulas, looking for the herbs of immortality. Many unscrupulous people take advantage of the situation and claim to be teachers. They compete against each other for clients. They do not reveal anything and they make everything appear mysterious. They take the false and present it as real. They claim to be experts of divination but they do not understand the principles of change. They practice the minor techniques of false teachings and present them as the ultimate truth. They try to make the real medicine out of ordinary metal, stone, grass, and wood. Failing to produce results, they have led people to doubt the methods of the golden nectar.

Translator's Note

Peng-lai is the Island of Immortality. In the center of this legendary isle is a mountain shaped like a jug. It is said that mortals who drink the waters flowing out of this mountain will become immortal.

32

Lodestone and Metal Are Attracted to Each Other

Lodestone and metal are attracted to each other even at a distance. But, compared with them, the contents of an egg are even more attached to each other. Coming together, they give birth. The best metal and earth are always with mercury.

Primary Commentary

Lodestone and metal are attracted to each other even at a distance.

The magnetic strength of lodestone is so great that it can pull a metal object toward it from a distance. This is because there is a natural attraction between them. The *Tsan-tung-chi* says, "Even when it is elusive and far, there is a connection despite the distance."

But, compared with them, the contents of an egg are even more attached to each other. Coming together, they give birth.

The chamber of the spirit is built with white metal and is shaped like an egg. Patterned after the union of sky and earth, it creates the numinous mercury when water and fire are circulated. The *Tsan-tung-chi* says, "It is shaped like an egg. The black and white embrace each other." Within sky and earth is the mysterious essence of the Great Yin. Inherent in all things large and small, its myriad transformations are reflected in the ten thousand things. The enlightened ones tamed and ingested it to cultivate immortality. Do you want to know how this essence is tamed? The key lies in white metal. Only white metal has the quality to control it and persuade it to stay and be transformed together.

The best metal and earth are always with mercury.

Metal is ch'ien and earth is k'un. When the feelings of attraction are aroused, ch'ien and k'un will give birth to mercury and lead. The two substances support each other. They become the golden nectar and do not fly away. The *Tsan-tung-chi* says, "Movement, stillness, and rest are always with us."

Secondary Commentary

The enlightened ones of old realized that the key to the subtle mystery lies in cultivating the golden cauldron. The golden cauldron is difficult to build. However, those who can make it will be able to gather the vapor of the ten thousand transformations and penetrate the essence of the golden nectar. Before things took on shape and form, they were undifferentiated from each other. Sky and earth were joined and shaped like an egg. If you can get to this origin, you will be able to attain the supreme way. The Tao was there before sky and earth were created. It is the beginning of all things. Of all the Taoist arts, the art of immortality is the oldest. Those who know it will live a long life. Their spirit will not be harmed.

33

The Emphasis on the Firing Process Is Not Empty Talk

The emphasis on the firing process is not empty talk. It is not an attempt to inflate the importance of this book. The methods of the elixir have been discussed elsewhere. Thus there is no need to enumerate them here. Therefore only the mnemonics of firing are presented in the text.

Primary Commentary

The emphasis on the firing process is not empty talk. It is not an attempt to inflate the importance of this book.

There are about six hundred treatises describing the firing process. The fire is to be circulated for ten months. There are thirty days in each month. There is one hexagram governing each day and one governing each night. Thus there are sixty hexagrams governing each month and six hundred hexagrams governing the ten months. The second and eighth months are governed by a special set of numerics. In the month of mao, water is transformed and metal is positioned. In the month of yu, water is circulated and fire is stopped. It is the same for the months of yin and shen. We do not need to describe the numerics further. They are recorded in the ancient text, the *Dragon-Tiger Classic*. The firing process has been transmitted orally by the ancient ones. It is not empty talk. This should be emphasized. The classics of the elixir say that "the ingredients are described but the firing process is not explained."

The methods of the elixir have been discussed elsewhere. Thus there is no need to enumerate them here.

The methods of firing have been discribed in the earlier chapters. There is no need to discuss them here.

Therefore only the mnemonics of firing are presented in the text.

This is an ancient text. The author is unknown. Those who have attained the Tao in the ancient times were afraid that the principles of the firing process would be lost and later generations would not know how to cultivate the golden nectar. Therefore they have left us this book.

SECONDARY COMMENTARY

People who learn the Taoist arts today often find it hard to get to the root of the golden nectar. They hang on to the crooked paths and are trapped in ignorance all their lives. Some sit and visualize images and some swallow the saliva while lying down. Some focus on the cavity of the Great Lake and concentrate on the cavity of the Grand Pool below the navel. Some sit in meditation, trying to listen to the sounds of the spirit, hoping to separate the lead and the mercury. Others take the interaction of the heart and kidneys as the work of water and fire. These are only elementary techniques. Still, some try to absorb the vapor of nature. Some use sexual techniques to gather energy, trying to inhale the elixir of yin during sexual intercourse. As a result, they dissipate their blood energy and harm themselves. Their bodies decay and become like ashes and dirt. These are all examples of straying from the correct way. If you try to progress, you will fall behind. If you try to hasten your development, you will be slowed. It is a pity that many people lose track of the real method and go against the celestial way.

This book is titled the *Dragon-Tiger Classic.* The dragon is the sun and the tiger is the moon. The sun and moon are the ancestors of ch'ien and k'un and the creators of all things. The sky is the body of metal. Its color is light blue. It encompasses yin and yang and harmonizes the four directions. The three lights and the two vapors circulate in it. The ancient people patterned the furnace and cauldron after the movements of the sky and the earth and the sun and the moon. They caught the lights of the two images and gathered the vapors of the dragon and the tiger into the chamber of the spirit to make the medicine called the Golden Elixir. Therefore they called it the way of the dragon and the tiger. Immortal Wei Po-yang said, "The sprouts become numinous. The dragon cries in the spring. Multicolored clouds rise to the sky. The tiger roars in the void. The wind shakes the four directions. The flames of yang shine in brilliance. The fire of the pearl rises up. Yin appears, mysteriously full and complete." All this is part of the natural order of things. There is only one principle in the making of the Golden Elixir. If you use the five metals, eight minerals, and various compounds of lead, or visualize images, or gather the elixir of yin, or gaze at the sun and moon, hoping to fly to them, you will make it hard on yourself. There are thirty-three chapters in this text. If you find variants of this text where some words are different, you should know that the words have been inserted by later generations posing as authoritative sources. These superfluous words have been edited from this text. Based on the *Tsan-tung-chi* of Wei Po-yang, the book is divided into thirty-three chapters. It is hoped that later generations of students will not lose track of the sequence of the chapters. It does not matter whether you live in the mountains and forests or hide in the city. All those who are deeply rooted in the Tao should look to the *Tsan-tung-chi* for guidance.

TRANSLATOR'S NOTE

Absorbing the vapor of nature refers to absorbing the energy of the sun, moon, stars, and mist. The Shang-ch'ing school of Taoism, which flourished between the fourth and tenth centuries CE, believed that one can attain longevity and immortality by "swallowing" the essences of the celestial bodies and inhaling the vapors of earth such as mist. The practitioners of Shang-ch'ing Taoism also believed that visualizing the images of the guardian spirits of the body will keep the spirits within and protect the body from illness.

Books by Eva Wong

Cultivating Stillness
Cultivating the Energy of Life
Feng-shui
Harmonizing Yin and Yang
Holding Yin, Embracing Yang
Lieh-tzu
A Master Course in Feng-shui
Nourishing the Essence of Life
The Pocket Tao Reader
Seven Taoist Masters
The Shambhala Guide to Taoism
Tales of the Dancing Dragon: Stories of the Tao
Tales of the Taoist Immortals
Teachings of the Tao

Printed in the United States
by Baker & Taylor Publisher Services